KENTUCKY IS MY LAND

KENTUCKY IS MY LAND

Jesse Stuart

with an Afterword by
JIM WAYNE MILLER

THE JESSE STUART FOUNDATION

Jesse Stuart Foundation
KENTUCKY IS MY LAND
Copyright © 1952 by E.P. Dutton, Inc.
Copyright © 1980, by Jesse Stuart Foundation.
Afterword by Jim Wayne Miller Copyright © 1987 by
The Jesse Stuart Foundation

Library of Congress Cataloging-in-Publication Data

Stuart, Jesse, date
    Kentucky is my land / Jesse Stuart : with an afterword by Jim
Wayne Miller.
        p.   cm.
    Summary: A collection of poems centered on family, home, freedom,
and work by a Kentuckian convinced that his native state is the
heart of the nation.
    ISBN 0-945084-01-3 : $10.95
    1. Kentucky--Poetry.   [1. Kentucky-- Poetry. 2. American poetry.]
I.   Title.
PS3537.T92516K4   1992   92-779
811' .52--dc20   CIP
                                                             AC

Published by:
The Jesse Stuart Foundation
P.O. Box 391
Ashland, KY 41114
1992

Foreword

Jesse Stuart was a great American, a true ambassador of good will for his Appalachian homeland, and a prolific author of more than sixty books and almost countless poems, short stories, and essays. Many of his world-recognized classics reflect the solid values of the people of his beloved Kentucky homeland. That, in part, is why the Commonwealth named him its first poet laureate.

Jesse lived in rural Greenup County, "just down the road" from the Ashland, Ky., headquarters of Ashland Oil, Inc. From the company's early days, when it was a small, regional refiner and marketer, Jesse enthusiastically supported Ashland Oil, Inc. He owned Ashland Oil stock and took a keen interest in the company, regularly braving Eastern Kentucky's January weather to attend the annual stockholders' meeting.

As Ashland Oil grew in size, Jesse grew in stature as an educator and a writer. Soon both the company and the man had gained national reputation and respect.

For these and many other reasons, Ashland Oil is proud to underwrite this reprinting of KENTUCKY IS MY LAND. Although Jesse is no longer with us, Ashland Oil believes that his works should live forever in the minds of proud Kentuckians.

For Ashland Oil,

John R. Hall
Chairman of the Board,
Chief Executive Officer

CONTENTS

I. Kentucky Is My Land   9

II. The Ballad of Lonesome Waters   19

III. Songs for Naomi   35

IV. Poems for My Daughter   43

V. Songs of a Mountain Plowman   51

VI. Great Lakes Naval Training Station   73

VII. The Builder and the Dream   83

Afterword by Jim Wayne Miller   97

PART ONE

Kentucky is My Land

Kentucky is my land.
It is a place beneath the wind and sun
In the very heart of America.
It is bounded on the east, north and west by rivers
And on the south by mountains.
Only one boundary line is not a natural one,
It is a portion of southern boundary
That runs westward from the mountains
Across the delta lowlands to the Mississippi.

Within these natural boundaries is Kentucky,
Shaped like the mouldboard on a hillside turning-plow.
Kentucky is neither southern, northern, eastern or western,
It is the core of America.
If these United States can be called a body,
Kentucky can be called its heart.

I didn't have any choice as to where I was born,
But if I had had my choice,
I would have chosen Kentucky.
And if I could have chosen wind to breathe,
I would have chosen a Kentucky wind
With the scent of cedar, pinetree needles,
Green tobacco leaves, pawpaw, persimmon and sassafras.
I would have chosen too,
Wind from the sawbriar and greenbriar blossoms.

If I could have chosen the spot in Kentucky,
I would have chosen W-Hollow,
The place where I was born,
Where four generations of my people have lived,
And where they still live.
Here, too, I have always lived where
The hills form a semicircle barrier against roads
And there is only one way to get out.

This way is to follow the stream.
Here, I first saw Kentucky light.
Here, I first breathed Kentucky air.
And here I grew from childhood to manhood
Before I had been away to see what lay beyond
The rim of hills that closed my world.

I followed the little streams
That flowed over rocks between the high hills to the rivers
And then somewhere into the unknown world.
I hunted the wild game in the hunting seasons
Skillful as an Indian.
And I ran wild over the rock-ribbed hills
Enjoying this land of lonesome waters, sunlight,
Tobacco, pine, pawpaw, persimmon, sawbriar, greenbriar and
    sassafras.
I enjoyed the four seasons,
Sections of time my father used to divide his work for the year,
As much as any boy in America ever enjoyed them.

For Kentucky has four distinct seasons.
I learned this in childhood
And I didn't get it from a book.
Each season I learned was approximately three months.
Kentucky wasn't all summer, all autumn, all winter or spring.
The two seasons that I wanted to be longer and longer
Were the Kentucky spring and autumn.

When winter began to break, snow melted
And ran down the little channels on the high hills.
Spring was in the wind.
I could feel it.
I could taste it.
I could see it.
And it was beautiful to me.
Then came the sawbriar and the greenbriar leaves
And the trailing arbutus on the rock-ribbed hills.

Next came the snowwhite blossoms of percoon in the coves,
Then came the canvas-topped tobacco beds,
White strips of fortune on each high hill slope.
Then came the dogwood and the wild crabapple blossoms,
White sails in the soft honey-colored wind of morning
And red sails of the flowering redbud,
Stationary fire hanging in the soft mellow wind
Of evening against the sunset. . . .
The weeping willow, stream willow, and pussy-willow
Loosed their long fronds to finger the bright wind tenderly.
Then came soft avalanches of green beech tops
In the deep hollows that hid the May-apple,
Yellowroot, ginseng, wild sweet williams, babytear and phlox.
When I learned Kentucky springs
Could not go on forever,
I was sick at heart.

For summer followed with work on the high hills.
I plowed the earth on steep slopes
And hoed corn, tobacco, cane, beside my strong mother
With a bright-worn gooseneck hoe.
Summer brought good earthy smells
Of tobacco, cane and corn and ferny loam and growing roots.
Summer brought berries too
That grew wild in the creviced rocks,
On the loamy coves and in the deep valleys.
Here grew the wild blackberries, strawberries, raspberries and
    dewberries.
All I had to do was take my bucket and pick them.

Then came the autumn with hazelnuts ripening on the pasture
    bluffs
Along the cattle paths and sheep trails.
The black walnuts, white walnuts, hickory nuts, beech nuts
Fell from the trees in little heaps.
And the canopy of leaves turned many colors
After the first sharp frost had fallen

And the soft summer wind turned cool and brittle
And the insect sounds of summer became a lost murmur
Like the dwindling streams.
Autumn brought sweet smells of the wild possum grapes
And the mountain tea berries
And the blood-red sassafras and persimmon leaf . . .
Autumn brought the mellow taste of the persimmon
That after frost did not pucker my mouth with summer
    bitterness.
October pawpaws with purple-colored skins,
I found in heaps beneath the trees when I went after cows.
I opened them to find the cornmeal-mush softness,
Yellow-gold in color and better than bananas to taste.

These things are my Kentucky.
They went into the brain, body, flesh and blood of me.
These things, Kentucky-flavored, grown in her dirt,
Helped build my body strong and shape my brain.
They laid foundations for my future thoughts.
They made me a part of Kentucky.
They made Kentucky a part of me.
These are the inescapable things,
Childhood to boyhood to manhood.
Even the drab hills of winter were filled with music.
The lonesome streams in the narrow-gauged valleys
Sang poetic songs without words.
And the leafless trees etched on gray winter skies
Were strong and substantial lines of poetry.

When I was compelled to put poems on paper
They wrote themselves for they were ripe
And ready for harvest
As the wild berries, the persimmons and the pawpaws
As the yellow leaves and nuts falling from the trees.
Then I went for the first time into other states
And I knew my Kentucky was different.

As I observed the closeness of the tombstones
In the eastern cemeteries
This gave me a feeling that land was scarce.
I saw the tall smokestacks of industry
Etched against the eastern skies
And cities that were a pillar of fire by night
And clouds of rolling smoke by day . . .
I saw New York, a city so large it frightened me,
Cliff dwellings as high as Kentucky mountains,
The streets and avenues were deep gorges
Between high walls of multicolored stone.
And while it interested me
To see how fellow Americans lived,
I longed for Kentucky sunlight, sights and sounds
And for logshacks and the lonesome waters.
I was homesick for the land of the fox
And spring's tender bud, bloom and leaf,
For white sails of the dogwood and the crabapple
And the flame of redbud in the sunset.
I knew that my Kentucky was different
And something there called me home.
The language too was different,
Not that it was softer
But it was more musical with the hard "g"s
Left automatically from the spoken word
And the prefix "a" supplemented . . .
I knew more than ever before my brain
Had been fashioned by the sights and sounds
And beauties of wildgrowth and life of the hills
That had nurtured my flesh from infancy to full growth.

Then I went beyond the hills to see
America's South of which I had always thought
We were a distinct part.
But I learned we were different from the South
Though our soils grew cane, cotton and tobacco . . .
We moved faster and we spoke differently.

The West I visited where land
Was level as a floor,
Where the endless field of growing corn
Was a dark cloud that hugged the earth,
Where the single field of growing wheat was endless, endless,
And the clouds always in the distance
Came down and touched the earth.
No matter how fast the train or the car ran,
It never reached the spot where the clouds came down to earth.
The people moved quickly,
They talked with the speed of the western wind.
They were "doers," not talkers.
I knew this was not the heart of America:
This was the West, the young strong man of America.

I visited the North where industry
Is balanced with agriculture
And where a man is measured by what he can do.
I did not find the softness of the pawpaw and the persimmon,
The lusty morning smell of green growing tobacco,
The twilight softness of Kentucky spring
But I did find the endless fields of corn and wheat
Where machinery did the work . . .
Beyond the cornfields and wheatfields
I saw the smokestacks of industry,
Belching fire and smoke toward the sky.
Highways were filled with traffic that shot past me like bullets.
And I found industrial city streets filled
With the fast tempo of humanity . . .
Then I was as positive as death Kentucky
Was not east, west, south or north
But it was the heart of America
Pulsing with a little bit of everything.

. . . The heart of America
A land of even tempo,
A land of mild traditions,

A land that has kept its traditions of horse racing,
Ballad, song, story and folk music.
It has held steadfast to its pioneer tradition
Of fighting men, fighting for America
And for the soil of Kentucky,
That is filled with bluegrass beauty
That is not akin to poetry
But is poetry. . . .
And when I go beyond the border,
I take with me growth and beauty of the seasons,
The music of wind in pine and cedar tops,
The wordless songs of snow-melted water
When it pours over the rocks to wake the spring.
I take with me Kentucky embedded in my brain and heart,
In my flesh and bone and blood
Since I am of Kentucky
And Kentucky is part of me.

PART TWO

The Ballad of Lonesome Waters

Come off the hill and quit a-cuttin' fodder,
Come walk with me, Dave, by this lonesome water;
Come walk beside your landlord's only daughter;
Come talk to me beside this Blue Creek water.

And one-eyed Jim he passes Dave and Liddie Bee,
He sees them spooning by a sweet-gum tree.
And Liddie's Pappie, Jim he goes to see.

And Alec Seaton on his hands and knees
Slips down among the pretty sweet-gum trees
And Alec looks and looks and then he sees

There by a sweet-gum and the lonesome water
Stood Lackey Dave kissing his only daughter.

The caw-caw crow he laughed from his tall tree
And never a merrier haw-haw laugh laughed he.

"O Liddie Bee, I'll plug that Lackey Dave!
I'll teach a fodder chopper to behave!
I'll put that scoundrel in a deep deep grave!
Above his bones the tall ragweeds will wave."

I am myself . . . I'll do as I durn please.
I'll churn no milk, black-flag no hound-dog fleas.
I'll patch no pants and stockings in the knees.
And from this yard I'll rake no blackoak leaves.

I'll let you know I'll do as I durn please.
And you can growl and cuss and storm and mutter;
Gather your apples and make your own old apple butter.

"I tell you, Liddie Bee, it'll happen soon
If you and Dave stay out beneath the moon
And lean against gum trees and spoon and spoon.

"We'll have one of them shotgun weddings soon;
You out with Dave this way beneath the moon.
This is the time of year of a mad moon."

O Pappie, Dave has gone . . . he went to sea.
He left a note down in a hollow tree.
O Dave he's gone and he did lie to me.
O what am I to do . . . oh can't you see!
Since my Davey has lied . . . plum lied to me!

The dead leaves in the fall-time winds are sighing,
High in the blue sky wild geese are flying . . .
I tighten my lips to keep from crying,
I cannot stand their lonely honk-honk crying.

What will the neighbors think of me a lady
Not married and going to have a baby?

I see the geese high in the blue blue sky.
They're flying fast with many a honking cry,
I think of Dave . . . I bite my lips and cry.

I know if Dave was here he would not cry.
He'd take his gun and them wild geese would die.
And married now, late in the bed we'd lie.
Lordie . . . I want to face the stars and cry.

I want to hide my face . . . I want to die.
It's bitter here . . . back here, I sit and cry.
I listen to the lone winds sigh and sigh.
I watch the winter birds come flocking nigh.

"My Liddie Bee, shore as them waters run
I'll get that Dave at the pint of this old gun.
I knowed he'd do this after your heart he'd won.
And now you bear for him a twelve-pound son.

"He will come back to drink of lonesome water
And hear Kentucky winds blow through the fodder.

"As shore as God has made the stars and sun,
I'll get that Dave at the pint of this old gun."

Dave will come back . . . I think it all the time
For in them lonesome waters, Pappie, he drapped a dime.
Dave will come back and then there'll be a time.

But, Pappie, what d'y know old One-eyed Jim
At the Buck Run dance asked me to marry him.

"A son by Dave, your chances are now slim.
Old One-eyed Jim . . . you'd better marry him
Before your hair turns gray and eyes grow dim.
Old One-eyed Jim, you may think lots of him."

And now beside the lonesome Blue Creek waters
Play Dave's son and One-eyed Jim's five daughters;
And Liddie warns them not to play close the waters.

The lazy hound-dogs snore and cuff the fleas
Under the shade of bushy cherry trees . . .
And the wind goes a-whispering through the leaves.
And Liddie Bee and One-eyed Jim are hoeing peas.

Nine years and Dave comes marching back in blue.
He says, "Where is the girl I loved so true?
Liddie Bee . . . oh, Liddie Bee! Oh where are you?"

And when dead leaves are strewn on lonesome waters
And fall-time winds were shaking blades of fodder,
Dave went to see old Seaton's only daughter.

He had come back to drink of lonesome waters
And take his bride, the landlord's only daughter.
What did he care for One-eyed Jim's five daughters?

And when Dave reached her lonesome log-shack place
He saw the marks of time on Liddie's face.
Days hoeing on the hills had left their trace,
Nine years child-bearing had changed her lovely face.
But Dave caught Liddie Bee in strong embrace
And put three dozen kisses on her face.

A gun went off and Dave had lost one arm
But then it did not do his body harm.
It would now be a little hard to farm;
To hold the plow with only one good arm.

When Jim came home he pulled a gun on Dave
But One-eyed Jim is sleeping in the grave.
For One-armed Dave was fast for One-eyed Jim.
He pulled his gun and got the best of him.

Out on a hilltop where it is so still,
Where in the moonlight sings the whippoorwill,
Lies poor old One-eyed Jim forever still.

Jim's cutter plow is standing in the furrow
And in his pea-patch ground hogs make a burrow.

Crab-grass is smothering the spindly corn.
The weedy place is snaky and forlorn.

When strangers pass this place so desolate,
Nine hound-dogs meet them at the front-yard gate.

They run up to their legs and whiff some scent
Then yelp and laze and yawn in self-content,
Their front teeth pretty as a monument.

The yard is green . . . it's like a velvet rug.
The sky is high . . . blue as a water-jug.
And through the air flits many a spooning bug,
And Dave gives Liddie Bee a one-armed hug.

In lonesome waters when you drop a dime,
It may be long but you'll return sometime.

Tall boulders scratched by wind and sun
On husky hill that shoulder to the sky;
Where water falls and rabbits shyly run
Is where Dave hopes his bones are left to lie.

Just leave him in these open mountain spaces
Where hungry buzzards circle low and veer;
Where wind's a blanket for dead warrior faces
And whines for each lone hunter lying here.

For he was built of stubborn mountain earth;
With kindred dust at death, let him remain;
He's been a brother to her since his birth;
Color was in his face and in his brain.

Then dig him a grave and shovel him under
And laugh and smoke as you do it, old friend;
He'll love the slash of rain, the sound of thunder
And the sunset of the coming journey's end.

I saw the cities and I learned too well
Each one can be a little piece of hell . . .
Yes, hell to me . . . how well I know they are,
Sometimes without a bird, without a star . . .
And cold-stone streets without the smell of leaves;
Even the wind there whips loose wires and grieves,
Grieves loud and lonesome over the white-hard street
Where click all day the passing passing feet.

I saw the cities desolate and gray
And children there without a place to play.
They were green growing corn the weeds shut in;
Tall slender stalks so lanky, pale and thin.
The sunlight did not kiss their death-pale skin.
And there was something smelly in the wind.

I am a lover of the earth and wind and sun
And I went back where lonesome waters run,
Where wind talks to the green leaves night and day
And children have some place to run and play.

And I came back to get a breath of winds,
Winds hot and fresh . . . fresh blowing from the corn;
Yes, I came back where high-hill blue begins
And grass and leaves drip fresh their dew at morn.

Yes, I came back where lonesome waters run
And where the white heat dances in the glen;
Where pasture fields lie sleeping in the sun,
Back where the slopes are tilled by stalwart men.

Back . . . back . . . I came . . . back to the midnight moons
That redden ember-like in blue-sky dirt . . .
Back . . . back . . . where whippoorwills sing dishpan tunes,
Back where the quails call night-time with quirt-quirt.

I came to lonesome waters in beech coves
That kiss the ferns and look to skies all day;
I came back to ten thousand life-blood loves,
I came back to the high-hill earth to stay.

I said: To hell with all the paper money,
To hell with nickel, silver, copper, gold . . .
But give me corn, blackberries and wild honey
And give me things that can't be bought and sold.

We could not stay about the house
Where so many were crying;
We pushed on through the sobbing crowd
From where the corpse was lying.

We walked the path behind the house
Among his blooming trees
And wondered if he dreamed again
Of gathering fruit from these.

His lank bay mules he used for plowing
The sandy upland loam
Played in the barnlot willow-shaded
Behind his mountain home.

His rusty ax stuck in the block.
In the furrow set his plow;
The calloused hands that used them
Were cold and lifeless now.

The bees he loved were working on
The tall wind-waves of clover;
The evening winds he loved to hear
Were softly blowing over.

DESERTED COAL-MINE CAMP

This is a place of desolation here,
Not any sign of life and all is still,
Except a blackbird on a berry briar
And lizard sunning on a window sill.

Sometimes a wind blows over with strange sound
Among these tumbling shacks where life once was;
The blue slate-dumps upon this pitted ground
Are monuments they left to wind and grass.

These paneless windows are dark hollow eyes
Of paintless shacks that soon will go to dust,
Where once within were children's laughs and cries
And parent love and kiss and mutual trust.

Where have they gone to leave their dead behind
In unmarked graves upon this lonely slope?
What way of life have these men gone to find
To earn them bread and give their loved ones hope?

In years to come their mother mountain earth
Will hide scars where these veins of coal ran thin;
Bracken and fern will lay a pretty wreath
To hide the sunken spots where mines caved in.

No one will know his dead is sleeping where
The sawbriars grow and rabbits nest and play;
Foundation sandstones soon will disappear,
Slate monuments will slowly wear away.

And those who went away will not return
To see this place of lost and shattered dream,
Now hidden by the bracken, briar and fern,
Between these hills, beside this little stream.

Rich dust from these decaying shacks will grow
Tall briars whereon birds will alight to sing,
And soft white petals from their stems will blow
Down leafy corridors of April spring.

I.

O clansmen, weep!
Mitch Stuart's dead!
Old age took him
At home in bed.
No Van Horn put
A bullet through
Mitch Stuart's head.

One war was not enough for him.
He gathered in his clan;
And warring in the black-oak hills,
They fought it man to man.
And old gin-drinking Mitch
He thinned the Van Horn clan.

II.

When old Mitch Stuart
Heard the brass band
On a parade day
Play "Dixie Land,"

On his lame leg
And hickory cane
He would step out
And march again.

His nineteen children
Dared not bother
On parade day
Their marching father.

His hickory cane,
His clumsy feet;
Would pop pop on
The home-town street.

But not again
His hickory cane
And clumsy feet
Will pop pop on
The home-town street.

III.

O thunder, pound your drums!
Pound, pound your drums! your big bass-drums!
For old Mitch Stuart comes . . .
His ox cart comes.

O lightning, cut the sky!
Old Mitch is coming to lie.

O oxen, roll your wheels!
O roll your wheels . . . your muddy wheels!
Under the rain's white spikes of steel
They haul old Mitch.

IV.

For him they pray
No lofty prayer;
The little crowd
Gathered there . . .
For him they sing
No songs of folly,

But by his grave
Six soldiers kneel
And over it fire
A farewell volley.

v.

Over his chestnutoak
Flies the wood crane,
Chestnutoak roots have grooved
His mortal brain.

Blue dreamer with ears deaf
To falling rain;
Blue dreamer with eyes blurred
To flying crane,

Do you dream you will rise again?

Blackberry briars are white with bloom
Where old Mitch Stuart lies;
Jarflies are singing at his tomb
Under the Blaine Creek skies.

vi.

If on his slab were carved
Something beside his name
And dates and regiment,
I know old Mitch would want
His epitaph to be:

Here lies old Mitch Stuart
With a bottle and a gun;
He's a-drinkin' and a-fightin' still;
He's got 'em on the run.
His feet are to the east,
His head is to the west . . .
No Van Horn's left to hit
The heart in his clay breast.

Old Mitch's a-fightin' still,
He's got 'em on the run . . .
One hand is on his bottle,
The other on his gun.

Much have I roved by Sandy River
Among the spring-bloomed thyme,
Where love and life go on forever
And where I've spun my rhyme.

Much have I loved by Sandy River
Girls with the light brown hair;
I thought love would go on forever,
Spring be forever fair.

The spring for mountains goes forever
But not for us who fade
In love and life by Sandy River
Before our dreams are made. . . .

Before our dust goes back forever
To mountain earth we've known;
Before the sweet thyme blossoms hither
Among the gray sandstone.

I pray the music from this river
Will sing for them and me;
Will sing for us, for us forever,
In our eternity.

PART THREE

Songs for Naomi

A SONG FOR NAOMI

Time has been good that you and I have known
    Since poetry paid for your wedding ring;
And we bemoan Time has so quickly flown
    Between our summer and beginning spring.

We were so eager in our springtime hour
    To build a little house against the cold,
To plant our yard with native shrub and flower
    And watch their springtime blossoms first unfold.

We work to fill our cellar and our bins,
    We work from spring until the freeze and frost;
We work against lean hungry mountain winds;
    We work to find our labor is not lost.

To know we have a home upon this earth,
    To have a little fire to sit before
And hear the crickets singing on the hearth . . .
    To have this much and still to work for more.

APRIL MUSIC

Naomi Deane has loved the music here
In early springtime in Kentucky's woods;
She always goes with me this time of year
To visit in the April solitudes.
No one loves more than she the wild primrose
That grows beside the lichen-gray sandstone.
She thinks it is the prettiest flower that grows,
But yet, I think, percoon can hold its own . . .
No plowman has a sweeter love than mine.
No fairer love than my Naomi Deane.
She climbs high hills beneath the oak and pine,
I carry her across the streams between . . .
She walks with me to hear the music in
The April torrents and the pine-tree wind.

HOW CAN I GREET YOU?

How can I greet you on your day of birth?
I cannot give you compliments on time
That passes like a young wind over earth,
I cannot pay you tribute with a rhyme.
I can't rejoice to see Time change your hair
Or take the April from your pretty eyes;
For you, my Love, are fairest of the fair
And Time, your enemy, I most despise.
I can go to the hills to pluck for you
Arbutus from the rocks, percoon from cove,
Flowers you love that April brings anew,
I've given you since you have been my Love.
But I can't give you praise that Time has flown,
You with spring's lilting beauty in your face;
I do thank God to have you for my own
To greet with April kiss and strong embrace.

LOVE SONG

How can I do without you? I cannot.
You keep our little house so clean and neat,
Each room with flowers in an antique pot,
Each bed, clean pillowcase and snow-white sheet.
While coffee hot, with eggs our hens do lay,
And wild grape jelly, bacon from our farm
Make us a good beginning for the day.
A small fireplace does keep our kitchen warm.
The pictures on the wall have grown in place
As leaves on oaks; and chairs are placed aright;
The ruffled tie-back curtains, crisp in space,
Are white-robed ghosts reflected in firelight,
With good books everywhere for us to choose
When day is done and while soft music plays;
In love with you and home, I hate to lose
These beautiful too-swiftly passing days.

38

VALLEY LOVE SONGS

Here in this wooded valley, mossy, cool,
Where mountain water murmurs over stone,
The jarfly sings upon a greenbriar stool
A song I do believe is all his own.
In this green mansion sunrays penetrate
The trembling leaves between the earth and sky;
The redbird sings a love song to his mate,
And lazy winds mock singing bird and fly.
To this green world I bring my Love with me
And leave behind my gun and hunting hounds;
And hand in hand we go as silently
As snowbirds over winter's frosted ground.
How can we sing a love song when we hear
The barking squirrel, the redbird's love-song voice,
The water, wind, the jarfly's lonesome churr?
We listen to the love songs of our choice.

TO CALL OUR OWN

A little piece of earth to call our own,
This little house that we have made together,
An open fire with seasoned wood to burn
To give us warmth against the winter weather
Are life securities we understand.
We know the strength and nature of earth's crust
Where we grow sustenance with our own hand;
Meadows we made and love and fondly trust
Give us soft flowering beauty in the spring
And long windrows of summer-scented hay.
Above our wheat the yellow finches sing
And pollinated wind corn tassels sway.
Dollars lose value, but our land will never
Where yellow finches sing for wheat-grain fee,
Where seasons come and live, then die forever
And sheets of honey-colored wind blow free.

WIND MUSIC

I'm thankful for a love who goes with me
When there is music in the wind at night
On mountains where boughs weave incessantly
Between us and the moon and pale starlight.
Immortal symphonies are played by wind
Of destiny that sweeps the upland cone;
Night wind in pines is a crying violin,
Night wind in oaks is a tenor saxophone.
Night wind in sassafras is a magic flute,
Through sourwood branches a soft-toned guitar;
In sawbriar tendrils night wind is a lute
Beneath the floating cloud, the moon and star.
We store a portion of this symphony
To live unwritten in our heart and brain;
We live a night of love and poetry,
A night of nights we hope will come again.

THE FLOWER GATHERER

I shall go out today and gather flowers
Or leave them if I choose still on the stem;
I shall go out and fool away the hours
Beside the murmuring Little Sandy stream.
And I shall go beside that stream today
To find a bouquet for Naomi Deane
Before the wind blows all the blooms away . . .
I'll gather phlox and mix primrose between.
This is the time to put all work behind
Since it is season of the bloom and bud,
When blossoms swell their fragrance to the wind
And earth and man are in a joyful mood.
Love in my heart and brain is revived now,
I haven't time to walk behind my plow.

LOVE BALLADS OF THE NIGHT

Sing out, great wind, love ballads of the night!
My love and I have come tonight to listen!
A fox-chased rabbit passes us in flight
Over the leaves where frost and moonlight glisten.
On Sandy's banks these tall gray sycamores
Are sentinels to watch my love and me;
Below us Sandy's rippling water pours
A song immortal as eternity.
But sing for us a ballad, winter wind,
We're tired of classic songs of falling water;
Sing us a ballad of our mountain kind,
Heart-stirring music we have come here after.
Sing music native to us mountaineers,
For years go past for us and love grows colder
And ballads are the sweetest to our ears . . .
Sing out, great wind, before the night gets colder!

OCTOBER LOVE

Your lips are red as mountain sourwood leaves
That hang upon the gray October bough,
Your voice is sweeter than the wind that grieves
Over this land alive with colors now.
Your pretty eyes have endless depths of blue
Like pools fringed by the bracken and the fern;
Your pretty face is autumn beech-leaf hue,
The fairest autumn color to discern.
What shall I do for you when autumn goes?
When sourwood leaves have fallen to the ground?
When cold snow-laden wind of winter blows
Through winter boughs unlike your sweet-voice sound?
I weep to think that autumn will be over
When winds have rained the beech leaves from the tree,
When mountain pools are under silent cover
And winter takes my autumn love from me.

CORN SONG

I.

I take my love with me at night to listen,
I take her on a warm night in July
When the bright full moon makes dewy corn blades glisten,
On a night when the soft wind hums a lullaby.
I stand by her amid this field of corn,
My arm around her shoulder, cheek to cheek;
We stand entranced until stars fade at morn
To listen to love words the corn blades speak.
The corn is like tall soldiers in straight rows,
The tall maturing stalks stand side by side;
Their tassels mingle freely when wind blows,
As if each were a bridegroom kissing bride.
A million corn blades whisper love is here
On these green acres that we cultivate;
With night enchanted and with heavens near,
We love tonight regardless of our fate.

II.

I take my love with me in somber autumn
When the wagon-wheel October moon is red
And wind frost-laden moans across the bottom.
We have returned to find that love has fled
And green corn blades we once heard whisper love
Are ripened by the autumn sun and frost
And rustle sharply when they're forced to move.
The wind will blow them thither to be lost.
The tall green stalks we knew, erect in rows,
Are broken at the top and at the knees.
We know this is the way that corn-love goes,
Caressing blades ride on each chilling breeze.
I hold my love in silence on this night
And our lips meet as they have met before,
Her once-brown hair shows signs frost is in sight;
With summer gone, we'll love in autumn more.

PART FOUR

Poems for My Daughter

POEMS FOR MY DAUGHTER

I.

This life that we created stirs in dreams
Tonight while floods of cold November rains
Charge down these rugged slopes in roaring streams,
And raindrops slither on our windowpanes.
This life that we created stirs beneath
Her quilt as if she were percoon in spring
About to burst from earth's warm loamy sheath
Into clean wind and sun where wild birds sing.
She brings pink mouse-paw hands from under cover
While her curved lips are spread in childish laughter
At songs of storm-filled streamlets running over
With dashing, splashing, cold gray autumn water!
These moods of mountains are a part of her,
Moods through eternal years that have been ours;
Too young to know, she laughs at little fear
In love with storm-moods in her cradle hours.

2.

Not only daughter of two worlds of flesh
But she is daughter of the new-ground furrow,
And daughter of the willow, oak and ash
And sawbriar clusters where the ground squirrels burrow.
Not only daughter of two worlds of blood
But she is daughter of the percoon petal
That waves in April wind in gleeful mood—
I think she is made of the percoon metal.
I know she's daughter of this mountain earth
For she was born with April in her eyes;
Her blood is of the land that gave her birth,
Her moods, the moods of wind and wild bird cries.
I know she is the daughter of these things
And I am not concerned with prophecies
To say in her are moods of many springs
And that she is as perfect as the leaves.

3.

While we keep vigil of this infant daughter
Through lightning and cannonading thunder,
Through lamentations of the wind and water,
I think of families now torn asunder,
Scattered and lost on roads with evil turning
While we sit safely here behind log walls
In warmth reflected from our wood fire's burning,
Safe from the wind and rain that sadly falls.
I think of quails that nest among the sedges
Hovering their fledglings through the storm;
I think of parent foxes guarding ledges
To keep their wayward young from hunter's harm.
Never before have I felt parent ties,
That comforts of a home can mean this much;
When not a parent, my roof was the skies
And homes were houses without living touch.

4.

Let her moods be the moods of blowing wind
That in this autumn rends the trees asunder;
Let her moods be the cooing doves that wend
To sheltering pines amid the roar of thunder.
Let her know winter moods so desolate
Of preening snow against leaf-littered ground,
Of plaintive bird confiding to his mate
And murmur of cool water underground.
Let her know flippant moods of mountain spring
That lift new tender blossoms from decay;
Let her know music of runlets that sing
With wind-blue water under dogwood spray.
These moods are musical to be instilled
In her small infant heart and plastic brain;
And let this tender world of flesh be filled
With clean imagination of the rain.

5.

Let her know rugged beauty inwardly,
Not artificial beauty second-hand;
Let her be free as mountain wind is free
To know, observe, and love her native land.
Let her touch rugged bark of sister trees,
Pull percoon petals and tear them apart
To feel and see the beauty that's in these
To make food for her growing brain and heart.
Let her know mandrake and the sawbriar tendril
And wild sweet-williams blooming in the cove;
And let her have strong legs to climb the hill
And let her have a heart and brain to love.
Let her blow milkweed furze across the meadow
And course each runlet to the valley stream;
Let her run for a spring cloud's shifting shadow—
Give her the world and time wherein to dream.

6.

I must be careful not to break her slumber
With brogan steps upon this knotty floor;
She must sleep through this storm night of November,
Sleep soundly to the music of its roar.
Too soon she'll know of greater storms than this
When she must be awake to know of life;
She must sleep now, know warmth and love and kiss
Before the days of work and dream and strife.
Her tender hands must clutch more than the wind
In days to come of living growth and dream;
Too many bookish facts will fill her mind,
Too much to see beyond this hollow's rim.
I know that sleep is good for infant rest,
This peaceful capsule of eternity;
I know that rest for her will be the best
Until she leaves this brittle infancy.

7.

Rest now, young brain, for dreams will break too soon
And shatter on your world like slivered glass;
These dreams will be as mists beneath the moon
And lonely as winds muffling autumn grass.
I speak to you of dreams since I've known dreams
And blood that flows in you has flowed in me;
I must warn you that dreams are dead flower stems
And sap that comes each season with the tree.
Rest now, for you have years of life to face
And many paths to walk beneath the sun;
You'll know the joy and sting of love's embrace
Before your travail on this earth is done.
Rest now, young brain, in tender brittle growth!
Be still, small hands, do not clutch for the wind!
Rest now, for many dreams will come with youth!
Be frugal with the life you have to spend!

8.

I hope her world shall be Kentucky's hills
Where lazy clouds go rolling out to space;
I hope she'll love the smelly sawbriar tendrils
And wind from them to kiss her sunbrown face.
I hope she'll gather phlox beside the blue streams
That hummingbirds and butterflies are after;
I want this carefree world to hold her dreams
While she is young and filled with April laughter,
I hope she'll run barefooted with the wind
As sprightly as young percoon in the coves;
I hope that growing things impress her mind,
That growing, living things will be her loves.
I hope she'll love to touch a tree, a stone,
That she will know each wild flower in the wood
And love the music of the night wind's moan
And breathe Kentucky's wind and know life's good.

9.

Soon as this autumn wind and rain subside
I'll walk through darkness under storm-drenched trees
Since thoughts stir in my brain I must confide
To earth and skies to put this heart at ease.
I'll hear fresh runlets singing with delight
Down slopes of rugged hills that cradled me;
I'll be kissed by the wet lips of night
While I think of her in her infancy
Cradled and pillowed down in sleep that breaks.
I'll wonder if dark hills will shut her in
Or if she'll find the rugged path that takes
Her out beyond these hills and moan of wind?
I know that over her are mountain skies
Around her are high hills in leafless wood;
I know her moods are wind and wild bird cries
And substance from these hills is in her blood.

10.

You fight, my child, against the time for sleep.
You listen to the clock tick time away
And watch the darkness over windows creep,
But you will not let go the passing day.
Day has been good to you, you've loved the light,
Your hands have been as busy as two bees;
You've read your books, dressed dollies for the night;
You have drawn horses, fences, flowers and trees.
Lie quietly; sleep is the thing for you
To build your body strong in growth and dream;
The morning sun will bring you time anew
To play beside the shining sunlit stream.
Too soon you'll know maturity and strife,
You'll spend your days like coins and spend them free;
This growth and dream of sleep prepare for life,
For growth and dream will shape your destiny.

11.

My child, your world is wonderful and new
And filled with beauty, strength and strange delight;
Trees bud and leaf and wild flowers bloom for you,
The sun is in the sky to give you light.
Good fairies come to visit you in sleep
To help watch over you, their little Queen,
While you in slumber voyage on the deep;
On waking, you tell places where you've been.
You hold no malice, not with anyone;
Your flowers bloom afresh and never fade
In silver rain and dew and golden sun
Because the world you live in, you have made.

PART FIVE

Songs of a Mountain Plowman

NEW LIFE

Now I return to woods that I once knew
And I lie here upon the leaf-strewn ground
With ear attuned to hear roots breaking through
The unadorned and winter-lifeless ground . . .
For I do know when earth drinks rain that soon
New life stirs in the ever restless roots
Of violet, May-apple and percoon,
And ears can hear their tender bursting shoots
As they reach upward for the silver light
Of blowing wind, of sun and moon and star . . .
I know their stems seek life beyond the night
And nether world where worm and silence are.
And when I hear them breaking clods apart,
God, flower, stem, and dirt excite my brain;
I hear their little sounds above my heart . . .
Great growth to make the earth rejoice again.

INDEPENDENCE

Heaven be thanked for acres I possess
Though much is sterile clay and bluff and stone,
Land that I hope to hold for life's duress,
Land that by deed and in my heart I own . . .
And I am grateful for the hard-earned knowledge
That I know dirt and what to plant and when,
Experience I did not get in college
Nor from associates in a world of men.
I know that I can always fill my table
From this lean land with these hands and this head
As long as I have strength, am well and able,
Let come what will; I have no fear nor dread.
As long as I have land, seed, working tools,
And get a season not too wet nor dry
And have a team of well-fed kicking mules
I'm independent and I'll do or die. . . .

HOLD TO A LIVING DREAM

Hold to a living dream if you have one
For dream is not akin to dirt and stone,
What is more precious here beneath the sun
Than human dream, this something that you own
Created by your heart and pulsing brain
At any hour, through death's throes of sleep,
Or when you wake and walk in white spring rain,
Or in your youth or when the late hours creep?
Remember stones will crumble, dirt will loose
An avalanche of dream in tender spring
To bud and flower into a luscious fruit . . .
Winter, this dream will not be anything.
Only your dream has value and can last,
This best your pulsing heart and brain did give
From your substantial or your shattered past
That flowered when you gave it breath to live.

THE TRYST

A mountain man I go while I am here
Because I have a meeting place with God
From time the sawbriar tendrils first appear
Until leaves carpet winter's lonely sod.
I go alone into Spring's reborn coves
Where wind-green blood stirs in the springtime flowers;
I cannot estimate my springtime loves
With whom I'll freely spend the fleeting hours.
Good late March steals allotted time of mine
When percoon buds explode in springtime glee,
When young spring wind is sweeter than old wine
And sarvice blossoms clothe the naked tree . . .
Then God gives me rebirth in April spring!
He puts songs in my heart I have to sing.

APRIL IS SPIRIT

April is spirit risen from the tomb
That winter held in cold eternity
Since autumn-death and devastated bloom.
Now, resurrection has set April free,
A light-green tender month with silver ways,
A thing of beauty from the bleak cocoon
To brighten us throughout oncoming days.
April is apple-blossoms on the moon,
April is honeybees on sawbriar tendrils,
April is eager packs of young clean winds
That ripple wheat and rustle leaf-cloud hills.
April is spirit and her beauty binds
Our hearts in unison of spring-clean love
Enough to make our winter spirits rise
Like tender percoon from the loam-rich cove,
Like singing birds into bright April skies.

TREES LIVE AGAIN

Trees live again in this immortal spring,
Dressed in their spotless shrouds of rustling green;
Song birds alight upon their boughs to sing,
In resurrected earth so bright and clean.
And sweet aroma fills wine-colored air
From blossoms on each gentle swaying bough;
When has there been a time one could compare
To spring's immortal resurrection now?
Short weeks ago this wood was desolate,
Its barren boughs gray ghosts of icy gloom;
Eternity of winter held its fate,
Without a tender bud, a leaf, a bloom!
How can we mortals doubt in heart and brain
We wake from winter-sleeping like the tree,
That we shall bud and leaf and bloom again
In resurrected immortality.

MAY I BE DEAD

May I be dead when all the woods are old
And shaped to patterns of the planners' minds,
When great unnatural rows of trees unfold
Their tender foliage to the April winds.
May I be dead when Sandy is not fee,
And transferred to a channel not its own,
Water through years that sang for her and me
Over the precipice and soft sandstone . . .
Let wild rose be an epitaph for me
When redbirds go and helpless shikepokes must,
And red beans on the honey-locust tree
Are long-forgotten banners turned to dust . . .
I weep to think these hills where I awoke,
Saw God's great beauty, wonderful and strange,
Will be destroyed, stem and flower and oak,
And I would rather die than see the change.

UPON THIS HIGH HILL

Upon this high hill where the rain clouds nestle,
Where snow is last to fade beneath the sun,
Is home of sawbriar, wild rose, Scottish thistle
And bracken flourishing where freshets run.
Upon this hill infertile land is thin
Among ravines, recessions, folded rocks
Where there's incessant blowing of the wind,
But it is home to possum, hawk and fox.
Tough-butted white oaks easily survive;
Persimmon, dogwood and the sourwood cling
Tenaciously to these rock ribs to live
And leaf and blossom for an unseen spring.
This land gives fresher beauty to the rose,
Land in the wind near sky and sun and star;
Gives autumn colors unsurpassed by those
Rich valleys where the soil and seasons are.

HER WORK IS DONE

I thought my mother was a forceful river
When as a child I walked along beside;
I thought that life for her would be forever,
That she would give me counsel, be my guide.
She gave me counsel as the years went by;
She taught me how to use a heavy hoe
On mountain slopes that shouldered to the sky
In stalwart corn and long tobacco row . . .
And as I grew in strength to meet the years,
Among the clouds, up with the mountain wind
She would not have me bow to petty fears,
She taught me courage that was hard to bend. . . .
Now time has passed with many seasons flown,
On mountain slopes my mother's work is done;
That forceful stream that was my mother's own
Flowed quietly toward the set of sun.

PRAYER FOR MY FATHER

Be with him, Time, extend his stay some longer,
He fights to live more than oaks fight to grow;
Be with him, Time, and make his body stronger
And give his heart more strength to make blood flow.
He's cheated Death for forty years and more
To walk upon the crust of earth he's known;
Give him more years before you close the door.
Be kind to him—his better days were sown
With pick and shovel deep in dark coal mine
And laying railroad steel to earn us bread
To carry home upon his back to nine.
Be with him, Time, delay the hour of dread.
Give him the extra time you have to spare
To plod upon his little mountain farm;
He'll love some leisure days without a care
Before Death takes him gently by the arm.

STAND OUT AND COUNT

Stand out and count tonight the winds that blow,
Stand out and count the times the green leaves stir
While earth is liquid-green and stars seem low . . .
Stand out and count, it does not matter where.
And you will see as often as wind blows
Are segments of clean beauty on this earth . . .
High clouds, moon, stars, mist, river, fern and rose.
    These things of beauty you have known from birth.
    More often than you count earth's heart pumps blood
    Through tight veins of the many rough-barked trees
    To give them life, leaf, beauty, bloom and bud,
    To give their rugged bodies symmetry . . .
    Feel in the vibrant wind earth's beating heart,
    Rejoice for life, love and eternity;
    And know that all of this you are a part
    Of everything there is and is to be.

SPRING SONG

In green-up time our fathers go afield
To plow the stubborn slopes their fathers plowed;
Planting in green-up time gives greater yield,
They work in sun beneath the wind and cloud.
In green-up time our mothers walk by streams
To pick the water-cresses from creek bottom;
Sallets are good for blood and good for dreams
From green-up time until the early autumn.
The green-up time is when our winter blood
Does change from winter-thickness to spring-thin
When we and earth are in a gayer mood
Than violets stirred by an April wind.
Our lovers walk the honeysuckled lanes,
In green-up time they never can love more;
They love in golden suns and silver rains
As parents loved in green-up times before.

MULE'S WAY

Before sunup I used to take my mule
To plow on rooty slopes of rot-leaf loam,
While sunless morning wind was fresh and cool,
And while we plowed my mule would think of home.
My well-fed mule would bend down to his knees
And stop the plow to get a bite of grass;
He'd stop at sounds of rustling April leaves
And for snakefeeders on their wings like glass.
And when he heard the distant dinner bell,
He would not take the furrow to the end
But he would stand a mule immovable;
The will of any mule is hard to bend.
Trace-chains unfastened from the singletree,
I'd climb upon his back and give him rein;
To ride this mule was an uncertainty
As we went home for dinner up the lane.

THEIR ANCIENT LOVE IS WRITTEN IN THIS DUST

Their ancient love is written in this dust
Of Flying Cloud and Princess Morning Star;
At last the plow has reached their final tryst
And sandbriar roots have sapped the dust they are.
He sleeps, a broken arrow in his skull,
In the cornfield by the waters of Siloam;
Her beads and bracelets are still beautiful,
Their bones preserved and bleached by sands of home.
Where did pursuit of happiness take these
When sunlit Siloam waters lapped the shore
And young spring winds sang in the willow leaves?
On red-moon nights what Gods did they implore?
And by some rival chieftain was he slain?
Was she once lovely? How did she meet harm?
Her face upturned to roots and summer rain,
She's found, through time, assurance on his arm.

CLAY FROM THE HEART OF IT

This is the land where wild persimmons grow,
It is the land of pawpaws, spruce and phlox;
This is the land where bloodroot blossoms blow
In early spring beside the lichen rocks.
This is the land where oak and ash and beech
Leaf early to the skyblue winds of April,
Where poplar trees grow to the low cloud's reach;
This is the land of deep ravine and hill.
This is my land and I am part of it,
Akin to everything hereon that grows;
I think I'm clay from in the heart of it,
My blood its rivers, breath its wind that blows . . . .
A cloud of green now hides its rocky scars.
It sleeps beneath Kentucky sun and stars.

THE UNDEFEATED

Only defeated and those needing rest
Recount the splendor of the sundown past
In idle dreams, thinking it was the best
And are regretful that it could not last.
The past a flame, how can the future hold
A million future dreams men hope will pass,
The bluer skies where rainbows will unfold,
Tomorrow's meadows with the lusher grass . . .
The future is a germinating seed,
A pollinating wind in thorn and rose . . .
Then how can such be cure-all for our need.
This dream, as time goes on, that only grows?
Remember Time the Present is here now,
The realistic dream we can't escape;
We hold it in our hand and when and how
Will you and I forge it into a shape?

WITH MUCH OR LITTLE

Rooted in my good earth like any oak,
Whose roots go down and cling tenaciously,
I have and can survive the blackjack stroke,
The lash of tongue, the whip of infamy.
And like the oak can live in sterile soil,
Receive so little nutriment for growth;
I learned to get life's sustenance by toil,
To build my body sturdy in my youth.
My flesh grew from the same earth-sustenance
That gave the oak tough fiber to withstand,
The lash of wind, sleet, drought and endurance
As much as any tree upon this land.
Rooted in richer earth, I still survive
When those who tried to fell me failed their task;
With much or little nutriment I'll live.
What more than this can any poet ask?

THE PLUM GROVE OAKS

There is no other tree like Plum Grove oak
Surviving on high ridgelines near the sky,
Recipient of the lightning's mighty stroke,
With branches, harp strings, for winds passing by.
Cool silver rivers of these high winds kiss
The soft leaf lips on straight and twisted bough,
And not one leaflip will these high winds miss
As they roar over starlit Plum Grove now.
The kiss of wind and leaf we love to hear
Among these oaks on Plum Grove's rough terrain;
From summer leaf until spring buds appear
We love the poetry in each refrain.
Today, I am the master of this tree,
To chop it down, to split its fibered seams;
Tomorrow, Plum Grove oak will cover me
And its tenacious roots will break my dreams.

I DO NOT COUNT THE HOURS

My pasture slopes have grown with sprouts until
Their spreading roots have choked the tender grass;
Each day I fight them with a stubborn will,
Persimmon, hickory, oak and sassafras . . .
I grub the hickory root beneath the swell,
I shrub the sassafras with sprouting hoe;
My mattock slaughters oaks as tough as hell . . .
The soft persimmon falls with lesser blow . . .
My days are long! I do not count the hours.
And as days lengthen working hours increase.
When a farmer goes to war the sprout devours
And grass that he has sown must get release.
On frozen hills beneath the winter skies
My strength is greater than the toughest sprout;
I work with warm sweat getting in my eyes . . .
And I shall get these sprouts without a doubt.

UP SILVER STAIRSTEPS

Up silver stairsteps of the wind we rise,
Our great ship leaves the earth's substantial floor;
We climb up in the spacious moonlit skies
Behind four trusted engines' mighty roar . . .
Higher we climb until the lights below
Are golden eggs down in a velvet nest
And motor cars are bugs with lights aglow
On arteries north, south, east and west . . .
What does it matter when we zoom through space
Where clouds sleep on bright mountains of the wind,
When the full moon climbs through clouds and tries to race
And our ship cannot leave the moon behind?
Reach out and throw a rock to slow the moon,
Reach out and grab myself a falling star . . .
From Knoxville to Chicago is too soon,
To coast from Heaven down where world things are.

GOOD-BY, MY LAND!

Good-by, my land! Good-by to hill and shadows!
Good-by to water falling over rocks!
Farewell, my streams that flow by little meadows!
Farewell, my stubble fields and fodder shocks!
If I had chosen my place of birth
I might have chosen fertile, level space
And not these acres of upheavaled earth
Where mountain wind put color in my face
And climbing mountain paths that made me lean
Against the wind and lift my feet up high;
Good-by to paths and valleys deep and green,
To friendly mountain sheep etched on the sky.
Farewell to land I love as I depart
To level, fertile space that is less fair;
I'll search the album of my brain and heart
To visit here if I get homesick there.

RAILWAY STATION, JOLIET, ILLINOIS

How many people have I seen like these,
Impressive faces I shall see no more;
These people pass like autumn wind-blown leaves,
Their footsteps echo on the clean-tile floor.
I meet arriving trains while I am here,
I hear the laughter, watch the fond embrace;
Departing trains, I watch the falling tear,
I see tears stream down fair and deep-lined face.
I hear fond greetings and the last good-bys,
Between train-times since I am forced to wait
In railway station under somber skies;
My heart asks me: What is each stranger's fate?
Where does he go and when will he return?
If he returns will it be love and bliss?
Will she be waiting and will her heart yearn
For his embrace and Love's immortal kiss?

TO SEE KENTUCKY'S DARK HILLS RISE

I weep to see Kentucky's dark hills rise
Through mist beyond the broad Ohio River,
Black umbrella knolls against gray skies,
Low mountain monuments to live forever . . .
These are the mileposts on the road to home.
Wheels on wet pavement can't roll fast enough
For me to see the blue swift water churn to foam
Down deep ravines and over rocky bluff . . .
My heart beats fast to know I'll hear again
Songs of these waters on a winter day!
For lonesome waters always stir my brain
And I remember them when I'm away.
I count the milestones as this bus returns,
I'll soon be in our cabin by the pine
And part of lonesome waters and the ferns
And singing mountain heritage that's mine.

THESE HILLS I LOVE

This night a million stars pin back the sky
To make a jeweled roof above this earth
And I must go to hear the night winds cry
Over these ancient hills that gave me birth.
I will hear messages from whispering leaves
That grow from trees in forests such as mine
Where beech and birch and ash are friendly trees,
Where sycamore is neighbor to the pine.
For months I've been away from life my own,
I've heard the song of wheels against cold steel;
I've climbed skyward, trusting the motors' moan
Across the continent. And, now, I feel
The sweet true surge of life in every vein,
Here in this night with brighter stars above
With beauty, song and peace to soothe my brain
Among these rugged hills of home I love.

BUILDERS OF DESTINY

They lie, our pioneers, where highways run.
They lie where railroads go and cities stand.
Their brittle bones have been exposed to sun
And wind. Their bones are restless in this land.
What does it matter if their bones do lie
Beneath the turning wheels where millions pass,
Builders and dreamers born to live and die
Like white plum petals on the April grass?
What does it matter if their bones turn stone,
Their flesh be richer dust our plowshares turn,
Builders who made America our own,
Whose blood has fed the roots of grass and fern?
Dreamers and builders of our destiny,
They left their epitaph for all to read:
A land of dream and wealth and energy,
A land where freedom is the greatest greed.

MODERNITY

Before the hard roads came my legs were strong.
I walked on paths through bracken and the fern,
And five to thirty miles were not too long
On paths I knew by tree and rock and turn.
I knew in March where trailing arbutus
Bloomed under hanging cliffs and dogwood groves
And thin-leafed willows were wind-tremulous.
I knew where April percoon bloomed in coves.
But since I drive, my legs are losing power,
For clutch and brake are not leg exercise.
I cannot drive contented by the hour,
For driving is not soothing to the eyes.
The road's grown old that I am forced to see
Above the stream where water churns to foam,
Where great green hills slant up in mystery . . .
I sometimes see a bird or bee fly home.

SUMMER HAS FADED

Summer has faded from all living eyes.
It is a written book that we have read
With sentences of green beneath blue skies.
Each word is now a leaf of dying red.
We stand to watch birds gather for the south,
We watch them rise in this bright autumn weather;
And with joy in the heart, song in the mouth,
They are off through boundless skies together.
Above the thistle furze that floats on wind,
Above the leaves of scarlet-red and gold,
Above treetops the autumn winds have thinned
They rise to sing before their autumn blood grows cold.
We stand below to listen and to look
And wait the season of another book.

THIS FEBRUARY NIGHT

This February night when all is still
Is not the night for one to lie in bed,
Not when cool starlight floods the winter hill,
Not when earth is so beautifully dead . . .
These stars have never been as bright before
When a sickle moon went tumbling down the sky;
The frosted leaves gleam on earth's frozen floor
And on these golden leaves frost-diamonds lie.
Stars in my eyes, frost-diamonds on my shoes
And sparkling beauty everywhere around;
So many winter lyrics I can't choose,
Even to water mummying underground.
I speak to the water and it answers me:
Record your little rhyme for those asleep
For spring will wake soon after February
And winter unrecorded will not keep.

THE GREAT WHITE SILENCE

The great white silence hides this barren land
Save blue chilled streams that vein this spotless white;
They mummy songs one cannot understand
As they flow icily into the night . . .
This night is dream-stuff colorful and still
Save for mice cutting in the foddershocks
And a hootowl's hooting from a great white hill
And foxes rattling dry leaves under rocks . . .
This cold blue night each star is set in place
And each star is a golden pin to hold the sky
Up in its high illimitable space,
A thing of beauty for a poet's eye . . .
To live and be a part of poetry
On a night like this that might not come again
Is something near to immortality
This poet's words can't capture and retain.

DEAD LEAVES REMIND US TIME IS LATE

The frost has brought this summer to an end,
Enchanted summer filled with growth and dream;
Over these wooded hills and wind puffs send
The multicolored rain on earth and stream.
Hereon this dwindling stream I watch a drop
Go like a galleon on the Spanish Main;
I wonder where and if that it will stop
And if our summer days are leaves of rain
Now current-carried, hither, thither blown
Over the dying earth so desolate
Into a winter death strange and forlorn!
Why do dead leaves remind us time is late?
Leaves are as hours that strangely disappear
When frost has brought good summer to a close;
We know it by the somber songs we hear
Of crickets, dwindling streams and wind that blows.

THE TIME OF FROST

It is too late for beetles now to sing,
Too late for butterflies to drink from flowers;
Now is the time for hunters' guns to ring
In these brown autumn leafstrewn woods of ours.
The chill has come and caught us unaware
For frosts have nipped the corn and cane and burley;
Two weeks ago the days were warm and fair
But unexpected frost came very early . . .
The rabbits' fur has changed from gray to brown,
The color of ripe leaves beneath the sun;
They feed when soft moon-misted leaves rain down.
Night brings them refuge from the hunter's gun.
This is the time of frost and wild bird cries;
The time of ripe leaves and blue windy skies.

A TREE THAT MEN WILL SLAY

The dogwood is a tree that men will slay
To make the ugly runners for a sled
Because its wood is slow to wear away . . .
Its wood is durable alive or dead . . .
The dogwood is the prettiest tree I know
To see its cold gray fingers in the spring
Loaded with blossoms white as sunlit snow
With birds among these boughs to nest and sing.
Its beauty is enough to lift the heart
When the early April world is bleak and cold;
Its autumn leaves are slowest to depart,
It stands a cone of clean wind-rustling gold.
And when the leaves depart the blood-red seed
Adorn each bough of iron tracery
And robins flock to this delicious feed
To strip the boughs and leave a naked tree.

THE PAWPAW

Down in the valley where the leaf-rot loam
Is near the brink of ever-flowing water,
The pawpaw springs up from this natural home,
One sprout will spring and then a grove come after.
Their copper-colored blooms are first to show
When other boughs are barren of the leaf;
Before wildplums are white with blooming snow,
The pawpaws' blooming season has been brief.
Soon in green clusters pawpaw fruit does swell
Beneath the leaves that hide it from the sun;
Perpetual water, loam, sustain it well
Until the summer growing season's done . . .
Then autumn frost will ripen golden-yellow
This most delicious of all wildwood fruit
That falls on pawpaw leaves for earth to mellow
For hungry man and bird and beast to loot.

WHERE THE AUTUMN GOES

Why stand and wonder where the autumn goes,
Each year one goes somewhere into the past;
Its golden goes with every wind that blows,
For autumn is a color that can't last . . .
And years are pages in an autumn book,
Each season's passing is a written page;
And if you can turn back the page to look
At Time's recording of each little age . . .
Turn mellow pages of the autumn gone
Where winds rain leaves on some familiar street;
Go back into a world you have not known
And listen to the sounds of passing feet.
You'll find the sounds the same that time and now
And autumn songs of wailing winds the same.
Then what's the use to question where and how
An autumn goes or future whence it came?

69

THIS CHANGE TO WINTER

This change to winter brings my heart relief,
I who did weep with autumn while it tarried;
The wind and dying leaf brought only grief
That winter has so comfortably buried.
Under a blanket that is clean and cool
Earth lies immovable in quiet sleep,
Beneath this blanket thin and beautiful,
While dreaming leafless trees a vigil keep
With watchful stars in a high blue bowl of sky.
And while I walk upon earth's sleeping breast
I am content to know earth's tired bones lie
In comfort and a much deserving rest.
Too soon the white hair roots will break dirt-skin,
Exciting earth into poetic mood,
And winter will go out and spring come in
With dream and blossom and new wine-green blood.

WINTER RIVER'S MOOD

Give me a summer river, not this one
That gathers water from high hills of snow;
Give me smooth waters rippling in the sun
Where bankside sycamores and willows grow.
A summer river has the mood of peace
That soothes my nerves and calms my restless brain,
A solitude where days of life increase,
A place where I can find myself again . . .
To sit by water lapping on the shore,
To speak to it and have it speak to me . . .
To see leaves trembling on the sycamore,
To hear wind in the thin-leafed willow tree . . .
But not for me a raging, swollen river
With winter moods that stir my brain and blood;
I'll take the summer peace and live forever,
I must escape the winter river's mood.

I CANNOT WRITE TONIGHT

I cannot write tonight for the moon is full
And large as a wagon-wheel above the timber;
I must go out for the world is beautiful,
Must leave the open fire and dying ember.
For what are words upon an ink-stained scroll
When magic moonlight floods this stubborn world,
When wary winds of ruthless winter roll
Over the knolls, and leaves and sedge are hurled
Into illimitable starry space . . .
I must be out in beauty, hectic, rough,
On mountains big enough for my embrace;
I must be out where I can love enough . . .
Remember hills stay young; their beauty keeps
Eternally as seasons come and pass;
They will be here when this admirer sleeps
Who will not leave his shadow on their grass.

SASSAFRAS

The sassafras stands winter barren now.
Its leaves were torn away in autumn strife
By elements that conquered growth and plow.
Deep rooted in this earth, it dreams of life.
There was a season when it leafed in full,
When birds alighted in its boughs to sing,
A pretty tree, thin-leafed and beautiful
That woke from sleep to promises of spring.
This sassafras is tracery of bone,
Shorn of its summer green and golden leaf;
Out in this winter wind it stands alone,
Its naked branches whisper of its grief.
But it will only sleep the winter through.
New life will come again in leaf and bud.
My friend, when winter comes to me and you,
Will spring give us new birth, I'm asking you?

71

Today our little world is clothed in snow
Except for channels where the streamlets run;
It stirs my brain to see the brilliant glow
Of pouring high-hill streams beneath the sun
That plow like ribbons of white-molten steel
Down rugged valleys filled with blazing light.
I shall go out and climb the highest hill
Where I shall stay until approaching night
To breathe deep down sun-softened atmosphere.
My searching eyes will focus every scene
From redbird on wind-sagging berry briar
To snow still clinging to the winter-green
Of swaying pines on ridges near the sky.
I must possess before it does depart
This world of winter beauty born to die
To store for summer keeping in my heart.

PART SIX

Great Lakes Naval Training Center

GREAT LAKES NAVAL TRAINING STATION

1.

How can I keep my heart from flying home,
Rebellious heart that's always going back
To a mountain shack beneath the sky's blue dome,
Walled-in by stalwart pines, oak and sumac?
My heart knows cozy rooms, clean bed, and wife
And blissful love with joy of dream and kiss,
A tiny daughter filled with pulsing life,
Immortal things for any heart to miss . . .
Moon rays through windowpanes across the floor
And books disorderly upon the shelf
Are things my heart steals home to know once more
Since it must find contentment for itself.
My heart tells me to fight to end this war
And live these things I think I'm fighting for.

2.

Our shack remains protected while we're gone
Though closest neighbors are a mile away;
Deserted it will stand untouched, alone,
Until our coming back to it some day . . .
Even our bird dog is not there to see
That strange intruders do not come too near;
For bolted doors we do not have a key
To our possessions that we do hold dear.
Shack mountaineers vacate for war,
Uniting us against one enemy,
Will be protected by a service star
Placed on a window, door for eyes to see . . .
And for protection one does not need more
Than just a star upon his cabin door.

3.

I never knew before freedom could be
A little world of hills that I had known
Where I could get acquainted with a tree,
A sawbriar stool beside a lichened stone.
I never knew the song of April streams
Was sweeter music than the song of birds,
That old cocoons among the greenbriar stems
Did hold more magic than man's futile words.
I never knew how good it was to walk
In blowing wind beneath a roof of sky,
To hear the wind and tender oak leaves talk
Above my head as I went walking by,
Until first leave, nine days of liberty;
And then I knew how precious hours could be.

4.

Will your strength last to let you carry on
To farm these slopes that gave us daily bread,
To get along until this war is done,
To see our mules and cattle will be fed?
The little that we have can you still hold?
Our herds and teams? Can you keep fences mended?
Our land and teams are better wealth than gold
And we will need them when the war has ended.
Will you sow winter wheat on each creek bottom
And rye on slopes between the orchard rows
And plow our lots to keep the fires of autumn
Away from hay-filled barns and clover mows?
When this is over and I do get back,
With eager strength, I'll clear the slopes again,
Rebuild the fences, renovate the shack,
Replenish bins until they bulge with grain.

5.

When I survey the freedom that was mine,
Freedom as free as blowing wind is free,
I think of ridge-paths fringed by oak and pine
Where once I walked with wind for company.
Green slopes below were cool and beautiful
In light and shifting shadows of the sun,
And I could touch the clean clouds soft as wool.

This was the greatest freedom I had known
Where all the sounds were music that I heard . . .
The lyric laugh of water on the rocks,
The wind among the oaks, a singing bird,
And daytime-barking of the hungry fox.

> If I could choose my freedom once again,
> This kind I would not hesitate to choose . . .
> High mountain paths in mists and wind and rain
> With not one minute of my life to lose!

6.

When I remember winter in my world,
Good days of peaceful living stir my brain
When winter's barren timber twigs were pearled
With geometric frost, with drops of rain
That oozed down slick bark on the poplar trees
To drip on last year's leaves with "put-put" sound.

And I remember how among corn knees
Wind moaned above the sleeping harvest ground,
And in a groove beneath the ridge's rim
With axe in hand how I would stop to think:
Where's the best spot in this frozen stream
To make a hole for cows and mules to drink?

> I want this life with wind against my face
> Far from the city's ever pressing gloom,
> Where there are brother trees for my embrace,
> Pine-scented wind and cloud and elbow room.

7.

Are mountains peaceful in their winter slumber
Beneath their quilts of snow, of leaf and weed?
Do hungry snowbirds fly in countless number
Over the empty fields for ragweed seed?

Do foxes make snow-paths beside the rocks
And long dark trains of starving crows fly over
To search for frozen corn in fodder shocks?
Tell me, where do the coveys now take cover
From hunters' guns and foxes' preening eyes?

   I've been too long away from lonesome water
   And my log shack beneath the winter skies.
   Again, I'd love to carry bundle fodder,
   Scatter it on the greenbriar stools for cows,
   And with my peg split nubbins for the calves . . .
   Then watch them eat with eager foaming mouths
   The little quarter nubbins and the halves.

8.

Someday we might be going home to find
The weeds grown taller than our front yard gate,
Each window darkened by a lonely blind,
Dark eyeless cabin that's been left to fate
Except for wasps and bats beneath the eaves
And lizards running on the flagstone walk
And wind that rustles lazy dogwood leaves
Beneath whose shade our neighbors used to talk.
We'll give our cabin eyes to see again
When we return with chickens, dogs and cats;
We'll clean our grown-up fields for stalwart grain.
We'll clear the place of lizards, wasps, and bats.
Our chimney smoke will spiral on the air.
Old neighbors then will know that we are there.

THE LAST LEAVE HOME

I.

To see these rugged hills of home again
Before uncertain flight through troubled skies,
To be where autumn wind sends down red rain
Has brought me moods and hot tears to my eyes.
These are the jutted hills that nurtured me,
That gave me substance since my life began;
Within whose bounds I have known liberty
As much as any mortal on earth can.
I have stood here when other winds have blown
In seasons past to watch rain-dropping leaves;
Now I recount with pleasure days I've known
Before a change to scenes beyond the seas.
Upon this earth, beneath these clouds of fleece,
I wish I could command this time to stop
That I may know again these hills of peace
Where only leaf-blood trickles drop by drop.

2.

Upon this multicolored earth I stand
Where wind is in a wailing autumn mood
And briars catch leaves that drift across the land
That pour from tree-tops in a windy flood.
This is a lonely time to watch the leaves,
These many colored deaths that come again,
While minutes ride upon the wind that grieves
Across the hollow, jutted cliff and glen.
Unlike prolific spring when life was here
Among these hills with growth in bud and leaf,
This autumn's mood of death makes me have fear,
Makes me remember seasons are too brief.
Time is not long: "leave hours" too quickly pass,
Like these death-colored leaves that ride the wind;
Time is a speedy sand in this hourglass
Now that I leave this heritage behind.

3.

This flesh is substance of this dirt and stone
Since it was nurtured from a scanty fare
My father wrought from dirt he did not own
On slopes too steep and stubborn to compare.
I never knew how painful it would be
To leave this land with freedom of the fox
Where I have been a brother to the tree
Where there is elbow room among these rocks.
This blood goes deeper here than roots of fern
That clings tenaciously to rocky bluff;
These eyes have been quite able to discern
Upon these jutted slopes beauty enough . . .
These ears have heard good music from the streams
That carry lonesome waters from the coves;
Here is one place this brain is filled with dreams
As I stand here among my many loves.

4.

Alien atolls I know will not have trees
Such as the blackgum, sassafras and beeches
That are as tethered and as tough as these . . .
They'll have pandanas, palms on their small reaches
They will not have red-raining of the leaves
From clouded tree-tops with a preening sound;
Nor will they have an autumn wind that grieves
Among sawbriars close to frosted ground.
How can there be cool water good to drink
On these atolls scorched by a torrid sun?
It is enough to make one stop and think
As he stands where these lonesome waters run.
One can't breathe wind fresh-scented in the morn
By fingers of the pines and foddershocks
Where there are coconuts instead of corn
And coral studs instead of pine-loved rocks.

5.

Atolls are softer earth than stubborn hills
That do grow stalwart men of tougher clay;
Atolls won't have an April stream that spills
Over a ledge into a rainbow spray . . .
Nor will they have tough mountain paths to climb
That build strong muscles, make one's chest expand
For lowland walkers have an easy time . . .
Their muscles have the softness of their land.
Nor will their natives have a hillman's eye
Since they have been accustomed to discern
Only a little land, lagoon, and sky
And not the copperheads among the fern . . .
They will have flying fish instead of trout
And soft grasshut instead of hardwood shack
A season's sameness that may wear one out . . .
For a mountaineer there'll be no turning back.

6.

I would love freedom such as I once knew
When spring returned to hills, to coves and hollows
With April sun to drink the morning dew
And bright-winged butterflies above the meadows.
I would love airy April's spacious room
With wind washed fluffy-clean by thunder showers,
Scented by bush in multicolored bloom,
By sawbriar tendril, phlox and percoon flowers.
I would love freedom of the gold-winged bee
But not of minnows little creeks confine,
That I may walk forever just to see
Again this brain-embedded world of mine.
My heart and brain keep flying to this earth
That holds my past, my present and my future,
Whose April beauty fed this brain from birth
And whose loam gave this body growth and nurture.

7.

Remember if this man is lost at sea
In feathery fathoms of its midnight deep
And waves can't break my brain's last secrecy
These will be images that I will keep:
High rugged hills that shoulder to the sun
Where I went with my mother out to hoe
From early morn until the day was done
Light burley in the long tobacco row.
I'll keep old images of time and place,
Of redbud coves in fiery flakes of bloom,
Curve of Naomi's lips, her handsome face,
Jane's playing with blocks in our living room.
Eternal churning of the sea can't break
What I would sacrifice for freedom's sake.

PART SEVEN

The Builder and the Dream

When Ben Tuttle sat in the one-room Oak Chapel School,
(High on a hilltop above the other hills and valleys,
Where he could see his country from his windows)
He dreamed of himself leading a great army,
Great enough to conquer earth.
He dreamed he rode a white horse before his marching men,
And flags of many designs and colors
Rustled in the wind above his head like autumn leaves.
This dream ended when he read the fate
Of one Napoleon Bonaparte who tried to conquer earth
And whose six hundred thousand men marching behind his horse
Left their bones, picked clean of flesh, to whiten Russian plains.

Ben Tuttle once had seen beneath some sycamores,
Bones in the sun, with sawbriars through eye-socket rims,
With stained teeth and no lips to cover them.
Ben knew to lead men into battle was not for him.
It was then that he began to dream of something new,
To make earth better for his being here,
To help his people always and never destroy.
Always to build, ever, ever, ever to build,
To give a message, fulfillment of a dream,
To make a better home, a better barn, a stronger bridge,
To train his hands for greater, greater skill.

Then Ben Tuttle dreamed he was a railway engineer,
Behind a throttle, pulling the fastest train on rails,
A passenger train that didn't stop for little towns,
That like an unseen ghost his train blew past,
So true to schedule, when he whistled,
Men checked their watches to see if they were fast or slow.
Young Ben Tuttle dreamed himself into another engineer,
Who made great dams for water-power,
Checking rampaging rivers in time of floods.
His dreams were great in childhood.

And among his hills he had seen something
That made him sick at heart, something reminding him
Of Napoleon Bonaparte's destruction of human lives,
Something reminding him of white bones gleaming in the sun.
Ben Tuttle saw destruction of the trees which he felt
Belonged to him, these trees that were a part
Of earth he knew, had always known and loved,
Trees that were friends of his, and he thought would always be
In this great earth where they were born and nourished
As he had been nourished by food grown from this same soil.
Sawmills came to his hills and valleys as if lumber men
Had found these great resources of timber suddenly.
And there was the greatest slaughter of trees
Upon this land that man had ever known.

Bleached bones of trees with withered leaves,
Still clinging to the sapless dying boughs,
Trees, bones so dark-brown gleaming in summer sun,
Dark and rotting in the somber autumn rains,
Stark accents, no sound, when winter snow
Melted in early spring and flowed in clean blue streams,
Down indentations of earth and over high cliff walls,
Into narrow-gauged valleys to rivers and the sea.
Snow-water, awakening roots of these giant trees
Once drunk by gills, by gallons and by barrels.
Water that soaked into debris of rot-leaf loam,
Into the earth, thence roots of trees
And spring's awakening life of bud and leaf and bloom.

And now, in these vast upland cemeteries
Where shorn slopes, ridges, rounded knolls touch sky,
Uneven rows of tombstone stumps showed what once was,
Of the Nature-world Ben knew that folded in seven years,
While he finished high school and three years in college.
When Ben Tuttle returned from college, he wept to see
The last great tract of timber, slaughtered, gone,
With only unsound bodies of great trees, lying over the uplands,

Across the valleys and the dark sun-seasoned bones,
Of top, twig and bough, lying entangled over earth,
And young trees that would have grown to great trees,
Were stooped, bent, splintered with bark-scarred bodies,
Without future, looking to a blue sky, feeling root-pulse of earth,
Feeling the last earth, sterile substance, leaving their roots
As they were not strong enough to hold this earth
Their tall strong parent trees had held before them.
There was not the carpet of multicolored leaves
Knee-deep to man, ripened by frost and swished
To earth by October wind and November rain,
Leaves to absorb the rain and pack against the breast of earth
To make leaf-loam beneath the weight of winter snow
To build a soil-rind on the earth of great fertility.
And with the rotting roots of tombstone stumps
The soil gave way to spring and summer rains
And somber rains of autumn weeping for the trees.
Soil gave to streams from melted snow
In late winter and the early spring.
Ben Tuttle's heart cried out for something when he saw
        destruction,
Great gullies cutting deeper with each rain,
Leaf-rot loam fertility washed over cliffs
To narrow-gauged valleys, to rivers and the sea;
His heart cried for the tree, something magnificent,
Something substantial, great, he loved more than he'd known.

Ben Tuttle had found his dream, a thing to do in life.
He found it in the wastelands of destruction.
It was not something to write about
But it was a dream to fulfill,
Something to do with his practical hands,
To rebuild, to make this earth more beautiful
For his people and the people yet to come.
In his little stay upon this earth, to leave
Behind him something of value, something men would notice,

And look to him as much as if he'd been
The one who engineered the greatest dam in the world,
To hold rampaging waters of the mightiest river
For power, or to nourish roots of crops.

Oak Chapel was without a teacher, so he taught
And with his little pay he bought denuded acres,
These worthless wasteland acres on earth's face,
Acres men thought were ugly and of no value,
Decaying tombstones of trees and rugged cliffs
That shone like scaly monsters in the sun.
Ben taught the State's prescribed course in Oak Chapel.
He also taught his pupils something not prescribed
By his State's Department of Education.
He taught them something he'd not found in books,
Something his heart recorded from life's observations,
To build, to live, the substantial and the good,
To build, and live, and never to destroy.

And this, Ben Tuttle's dream, began with trees
That they might grow again in this wasteland,
And that his tiny checks for teaching school would buy.
After eleven years he retired from teaching without a
          bank account
But with seven hundred acres of denuded land.
And then he went to work to practice what he'd taught,
The lesson anyone, he thought, who has a dream should follow
To know that he is right before he sends his message on.
Ben planted black and white walnuts to furnish sprouts,
To set in richer coves where leaf-rot loam was left.
And little oaks, growing in fields men planned to plow
He dug up gently and reset to hold his slopes where oaks had
          been.
And by each tree stump, rotting now, he set a tree.
He left deformed bodies of discarded trees,
Scattered on uplands and across the valleys;

He left them there for a purpose, their log-rot loam
Was more nourishment for the trees to come than ashes.
He left the few young trees unbent, unscarred,
To grow up naturally from the earth and Nature's planting.
Ben Tuttle took away the damaged ones to shape, to build,
Fulfillment of his little dream of destiny:
     A great forest men would come for miles to see,
     A forest of and for the future men would need,
     After the wasteland.

If Ben Tuttle's hands were not skilled in the beginning,
They soon became skilled removing and resetting young trees.
Not any fires for him to burn the bones of old dead trees,
Left by the timber cutters, who worked for dollars, not the
     dream.
Ben moved these with hand spikes, to set a tree;
With these he filled eroded ditches streaking down the slopes,
Great ugly wounds in earth not good to see.
He did these things that did not pay him cash
To lay away for rainy days and to invest
In stocks and bonds, interests, dividends, collaterals.
His thoughts and dreams could never turn to these
For his investments were in sterile banks of earth
He owned by man-made deed recorded in his brain and heart.

Ben Tuttle made his livelihood by sowing grass for pasture
In broader valleys down between the hills
Where he had pleasant creek-bottom meadows to furnish hay
In winter for his cattle and lush grass for their feeding
From early spring until the frosts of autumn.
The grass roots held his valley soil to keep
It from the rivers and the sea while profits from his herds
Kept him in life's substance while he worked on
To build his forest back with trees, to build his dream.

Ben Tuttle looked to Nature's Book for guidance.
He reset trees adapted to this soil and seasons,

Trees, Nature had chosen over the centuries.
He planted oaks where oaks had been on slopes
And poplars in the narrow valleys where they'd thrived
And white pines on the slopes where there was poorest soil
And yellow pines on ridgetops where the skies came down to rest,
And walnuts, black and white, in loamy leaf-rot coves
And beech and sycamores beside the little streams,
Over his seven hundred acres of wastelands,
He salted earth with sweat while years went by.

Ben Tuttle's wasteland is the land of beauty now,
It is no longer called the wasteland of denuded acres,
Ugly ditches which scarred these slopes were no longer here.
The roots of trees have hidden all the scars
The avalanche of rain and freeze and thaw have made.
These roots go deep in leaf-rot loam
And interlaced so well they hold topsoil
Like threads hold the seams of a garment.
Ben's good neighbors, who once doubted his sanity,
Have bought denuded acres now since they
Observed what he has done.
They model for their future on Ben Tuttle's dream.

Ben lived to see fulfillment of his dream,
That cost him two-thirds of his threescore years and ten;
And he has loved these years because he found
The work he loved, growing in conjunction with Nature,
Millions of board feet of timber.
And cash offers that he had, have staggered him.
He could not have done as well financially
With any business as with this dream,
Which was not for sale.
Except when trees have had their growth,
They will be marked by a forester or by Ben Tuttle;
And when they're cut, others will be set to replace them.
Ben Tuttle will keep his forest mighty and intact.

Ben will keep his forest where the wild flowers grow in spring,
A spot of earth people drive miles to see;
Trillum, purple and white, May-apple and percoon,
Violets, white and blue, large wildwood size,
And trailing arbutus first to bloom in spring,
Growing from rock-shelves on high cliffs.
His lavender and white pansies grow on the ridge-tops,
And fields of baby tears beneath his mighty oaks;
Golden cinquefoil, growing from sterile earth beneath his pines,
Wild phlox, pink and white and blue under his sycamores
And beeches growing beside the little streams.

Wild roses around the cliffs in summer
Are haunts for wild bees that found homes
In his forest and nectar in his wild flowers.
Wild huckleberry, gooseberry and snowball blossoms,
Purple ironweed blossoms beside the streams,
And everywhere, spring, summer, autumn field daisies
And in late summer black-eyed Susans in the open spaces.
Oh, great wild land, how good to love!
How great to be a part and have a dream!
How great for everyone to see and love,
To leave wild beauty in their hearts and brain.
Even the flowers of autumn when leaves fall,
When green of spring and summer turns to autumn gold,
The white, blue, purple farewell-to-summer,
Nodding in frost-laden wind beside the streams and paths,
Tell Ben and all his friends that summer is over.
High on the sumac antlers, high above the blood-red leaves
The cones of berries red as a rooster's comb
Tell them another summer has come and gone,
Leaving Ben Tuttle's forest with accumulated growth,
In height and in circumference.
And one more layer of leaf-rot loam
To enrich the interlacing roots of trees and flowers,
Wild asters by the dwindling autumn streams,
Wild sunflowers, golden in October sun.

Where can man find a richer life than this?
To see each season born, to see it die,
To hear each day the voice of Nature speak,
To read each day her message in the sky,
On bark of trees, in blades of grass and flowers!

Never has there been a fire in his forest,
To kill wildlife, destroy flower and tree.
How could he stand to see the dream go up in flame?
Burned trunks of his trees when sap is high,
To leave charred hulks, stark accents, no sound.
In autumn when the summer season ends,
In springtime when the raindrops wash young leaves,
When Ben Tuttle planted the trees, he left great paths
Clean of leaf and tree up vale and hollow,
Along the ridges so fire could not cross,
Great paths whereby he could control the fire.
His dream must not go back to ashes,
His simple dream of destiny.
Squirrels have returned to his land,
To find home and to replenish their species
Where there is food on wild mulberry tree,
The hickory, oak, and sweet buds of the pine.
The raccoon, rabbit, possum and ground-squirrel,
The groundhog, mink, the weasel and the fox,
Have found homes in his forest unmolested.
They den in hollow trees, in squirrel-made nests,
In rock-cliff dens on slopes beneath tough-butted oaks.
The last wild refuge for their security.

In spring when beech buds begin to swell,
Ben Tuttle walks in his woods to hear the music in
The wind as it blows through the leafing branches
Of beech and poplar deep in the valleys.
He's heard the strong night winds struggle with
The tough, endurable oak twigs on the rugged trees.
He's walked the ridges to hear this wind

To look up through the tree-tops with thin leaves
To see the light-gold factual stars
Twinkling in an upturned bowl of blue.
He's breathed this good wind freshly scented by
Pine needles, fern, wild flower, bud and leaf,
He's breathed it deep into his lungs
And knew the taste was rich and good
As he walked paths and climbed the cliffs,
Intoxicated with the love of life and will to live,
He felt deep in his heart he'd followed Nature's Rules,
God had assisted in his dream and its fulfillment.
He thought this was the way God had intended
These mighty hills to be, these hills unsuited
To ax and plow.

Ben Tuttle found in his labors the greatest joy he'd known,
Labor of love where hours went by in unrecorded time;
For trees and earth and wind and moon and stars
Are great substantial things for man to love.
The lonesome music of the wind in pines Ben Tuttle loves
When a full ripe pumpkin-colored moon
Swims in the never-ending sea of blue,
Holding pine needles against its side of gold.
In autumn when wind rustles frost-ripened leaves
To earth in slithering rain, Ben walks
Beneath his friendly trees, touching their bark,
Remembering he set these trees in infancy
And how his soft schoolteacher hands grew calloused.
He walks in knee-deep leaves, fertility to his wild flowers,
And life-sustenance for his mighty oaks.
In winter when snow blankets these hills
And when his trees stand frozen in their winter sleep,
He walks beneath their barren boughs to hear the wind
Playing a lonely symphony without words.
He walks beneath his pines whose boughs are laden
With snow their interwoven arms and hands
Will not let reach the earth.

He walks beneath his tough-butted white-oaks
On sterile slopes where ledges crop,
Earth where only tough-butted white-oaks can survive
For it is great to hear a new wind music
In branches where dead leaves in winter cling
To boughs with their fiber tougher than the wind of winter.
He loves these oaks as much as man can love a tree
And deeply sympathizes with them because
They want to be evergreens so much
They forget each year to shed their leaves.
Ben Tuttle has these thoughts as he walks alone on winter nights
Over the dream he loves and has fulfilled.

To build with the substantial and the good,
To build, to build and never to destroy
One hundred thousand people lifted up
Until their eyes are level with the stars,
They have found Nature's book of rules,
And they have learned to read her language.
These are among achievements of Ben Tuttle's dream,
The richer part of its fulfillment.
He has the mastpoles for a thousand ships,
Telephone and electric poles for a thousand miles of wire,
Fence posts to reach across this State.
He has black walnut and wild cherry for furniture
(Not for gunstocks) and enough to build houses.
He has millions of board feet of oak, pine and poplar,
Enough hard and soft wood to build a small city.
And he has more than this! He feels accomplishment.
He walks proudly in the wind,
He has given something to his people,
To his country, his State and his Republic.
    He's done as much as the greatest engineer,
    Whose dams harness the mighty rivers,
    Whose skyscrapers reach for the skies.
    He's done more than a general who leads
    An army into battle for he has created.

He has done as much as the dreamer
Who sends his message to people in books,
Much as a composer whose symphonies
Are greater than the music of wind in the trees.
He has brought back beauty for the people
To see and feel and know,
To make them happier than
They would have been had he not dreamed.
He takes his place beside the dreamers
And the builders of our human destiny
Because he has produced a great forest.

AFTERWORD

When Jesse Stuart wrote the poem "Kentucky Is My Land" in November, 1946, he was forty years old and had been a nationally known writer, teacher and lecturer for more than a decade. Born in W-Hollow, Kentucky, near Greenup in 1906, Stuart had attended a local grade school, Greenup High School, worked in the steel mill in Ashland, Kentucky, completed a four-year course of study at Lincoln Memorial University in Harrogate, Tennessee in three years, and a year of graduate work at Vanderbilt University—all by the age of 25. He returned home and became Superintendent of Greenup County Schools—and the youngest superintendent in the state.

Stuart began writing as a high school student, and he continued to write and publish poems, stories, and essays as a college and university student. A "term paper" submitted to one of his professors at Vanderbilt University appeared later as a book-length autobiography. In 1934 Stuart took the literary world by surprise with his 703-poem collection, *Man With a Bull-Tongue Plow*. Other titles followed in quick succession: *Head o' W-Hollow*, a collection of short stories; *Beyond Dark Hills*, his autobiography; *Trees of Heaven*, his first novel; *Men of the Mountains*, more stories; *Album of Destiny*, a second collection of more than 400 poems. *Taps For Private Tussie* was a Book of the Month Club Selection in 1943 and winner of the Thomas Jefferson Memorial Award for that year. Stuart's writing had already brought him other awards and honors: a Guggenheim Fellowship in 1937 and the Academy of Arts and Science Award in 1941 for *Men of the Mountains*. The year 1946 brought a rich harvest of writing and recognition: a third collection of short stories, *Tales From the Plum Grove Hills;* a third novel, *Foretaste of Glory*. In addition, *Man With a*

Bull-Tongue Plow was selected as one of the 100 Best Books in America and one of the 1,000 Great Books of the World.

Stuart wrote "Kentucky Is My Land" not long after completion of World War II military service, and at the conclusion of a lecture tour through several midwestern and northeastern states. First the war, then lecturing had taken him away from home for a long time. He was especially glad to be back in W-Hollow, in Greenup County, Kentucky, U.S.A. The war was over, the enemy defeated. One time was ending, another beginning. It was time to take stock and reflect on the way of life that had been successfully defended. "Kentucky Is My Land," which Stuart had originally titled "Heart of America," celebrated this special homecoming.

As he considered his past, present, and future in the 220-line poem, Stuart's recent travels disposed him to see his beloved home state in its relation to other states recently visited, and in the context of the nation he had recently served. Stuart identifies himself with his home state. He sees Kentucky as the very heart of the nation.

> Kentucky is my land.
>   . . .
>
> It is the core of America.
> If these United States can be called a body,
> Kentucky can be called its heart.

Stuart celebrates his native state's landscape—its streams, rocks, hills, and rivers—and its four distinct seasons:

> Here, I first saw Kentucky light.
> Here, I first breathed Kentucky air.
> And here I grew from childhood to manhood.
>   . . .
>
> And I ran wild over the rock-ribbed hills
> Enjoying this land of lonesome waters. . . .

Stuart pays tribute to Kentucky as the source of his life. Kentucky is:

The place where I was born,
Where four generations of my people have lived,
And where they still live.
                .   .   .
These things are my Kentucky.
They went into the brain, body, flesh and blood of me.
These things, Kentucky-flavored, grown in her dirt. . . .
                .   .   .
They made me part of Kentucky.
They made Kentucky a part of me.

Stuart identifies the Kentucky soil, landscape and seasons as the source of his art:

Even the drab hills of winter were filled with music.
The lonesome streams in the narrow-gauged valleys
Sang poetic songs without words.
And the leafless trees etched on gray winter skies
Were strong and substantial lines of poetry.

Very much a Kentuckian, Stuart is at the same time an American:

I enjoyed the four seasons
        .   .   .
As much as any boy in America ever enjoyed them.

Turning from acknowledgement of Kentucky as the source of his life and art, Stuart sketches other parts of the country—"the closeness of the tombstones/ In the eastern cemeteries . . . / . . . the tall smokestacks of industry," New York City with buildings like "Cliff dwellings as high as Kentucky mountains." He sketches the American South, the West, "level as a floor," and the North "where industry / Is balanced with agriculture." Stuart is careful to note that people in all these other parts of the country are "fellow Americans." But no matter how great his interest in other American places and

99

people, he always longs for "Kentucky sunlight, sights, and sounds," for "logshacks and lonesome waters." And he concludes that while Kentucky is a part of the nation, it is a special and distinctive part. Kentucky's natural boundaries of mountains and rivers make the state something like a country within a country:

> Then I was as positive as death Kentucky
> Was not east, west, south or north
> But it was the heart of America
> Pulsing with a little bit of everything.

Kentucky's distinctiveness is the result not only of its natural boundaries but also of its traditions. Kentucky, Stuart writes, is "a land of mild traditions,/ A land that has kept its traditions of horse racing,/ Ballad, song, story and folk music." Kentucky's traditions render the state both a distinctive and an integral part of the nation, for the state has held "steadfast to its pioneer tradition/ Of fighting men, fighting for America." Since Kentucky is the "heart of America," Stuart's identification with the state is simultaneously a strong identification with the nation.

The subsequent sections of *Kentucky Is My Land* develop the themes of tradition, family, home, freedom, and productive work established in the title poem. Poems of part two, "The Ballad of Lonesome Waters," illustrate the traditional Kentucky of ballad, song, and story. Parts three and four, "Songs For Naomi," and "Poems For My Daughter," emphasize the growing importance of domesticity and the family for Stuart during these years. The Stuarts' daughter Jane had been born in 1942. Her presence impresses him with the importance of home and family. Now Kentucky is not only his land, and the land of his pioneer forebears; he hopes Kentucky will also be his daughter's land:

> I hope her world shall be Kentucky's hills
> . . .

I hope that growing things impress her mind,
That growing, living things will be her loves.

In another of the "Poems For My Daughter" Stuart describes
a stormy night when he and his wife Naomi keep watch over
their sleeping daughter. He contrasts the lightning and thun-
der outside with the indoor scene: ". . . we sit safely here be-
hind log walls/ In warmth reflected from our wood fire's
burning." He thinks of families "torn asunder,/ Scattered and
lost," of quail and foxes guarding their young from the storm,
and from hunters. He sees things as a parent now, as he says
in the poem's conclusion: "Never before have I felt parent
ties,/ That comforts of a home can mean this much."

The poems of part five, "Songs of a Mountain Plowman,"
point both forward and backward—backward to the compar-
ison of Kentucky's shape to "the mouldboard of a hillside
turning plow" in the title poem, and forward to his concern
with conservation of the land and its resources. In the poem
"Independence" Stuart sees land ownership as closely linked
to freedom, and he suggests that true ownership of land is
not only an economic and legal matter but also a spiritual
thing: One must hold the deed to land in one's heart.

These poems elaborate on his preference for the country
to the city, for the natural, organic world to that of the
planned, man-made environment ("May I Be Dead"). Here
he pays tribute to his parents ("Her Work Is Done," "Prayer
For My Father"). And as the seasons come and go ("Spring
Song," "Summer Has Faded," "Where Autumn Goes," "The
Great White Silence") he celebrates hard work ("I Do Not
Count the Hours") and considers the achievements of his
forebears. World War II, and in its aftermath the Cold War,
perhaps made Stuart more keenly aware than ever of the pre-
ciousness of freedom, of the gift of the land and its resources,
and of the accomplishments of the pioneers and settlers. In
"Builders of Destiny" he speaks of "Builders who made
America our own/. . . . Dreamers and builders of our des-
tiny."

In this part Stuart travels by plane, train, and bus ("Up Silver Stairsteps," "Railway Station, Joliet, Illinois"), considers the losses and gains of progress ("Modernity"), and as a result comes to appreciate home more than ever. His heart beats faster as he approaches home after a trip ("lonesome waters always stir my brain"); he anticipates becoming once again a part of his "singing mountain heritage" ("To See Kentucky's Dark Hills Rise").

In this group of poems in which Stuart presents himself as a mountain plowman, his concern for trees comes to the forefront. He thinks of himself as a "brother to the tree" and pictures himself "rooted in my good earth like any oak." His physical strength and certain qualities of character (toughness and tenacity) are the result of his body's having been nourished by the same soil "That gave the oak tough fiber to withstand" ("With Much or Little"). He writes of "The Plum Grove Oaks" that will one day shade his grave, and deplores the cutting of beautiful trees such as the dogwood ("A Tree That Men Will Slay").

The poems of part six, "Great Lakes Naval Training Station," further elaborate themes already established. These poems express Stuart's homesickness and his heightened appreciation of home and family. The regimentation and restrictions of military life stand in sharp contrast to the comforts and freedom he enjoyed at home. He hears the call of "lonesome waters" and imagines the life he has left behind: ". . . cozy rooms, clean bed, and wife/ And blissful love with joy of dream and kiss,/ A tiny daughter filled with pulsing life." Stuart associates freedom with his Kentucky home, and connects his military service with defense of that freedom. He concludes the first poem of this part: "My heart tells me to fight to end this war/ And live these things I think I'm fighting for." And in the section's final poem, considering the possibility of his death in combat, he again returns to a picture of home and family and freedom: Even if he should drown at sea he will remember the Kentucky hills, going out to work with his mother, redbuds in spring, his beautiful wife, their daughter "playing with blocks in our living room." These images would remain, even if he should be lost at sea, he believes, for "Eternal churning of the sea can't break/ What I would sacrifice for freedom's sake."

Stuart's concern with land, family, and freedom naturally involves a concern for the future. And in "The Builder and the Dream," the long narrative poem which constitutes the seventh and concluding part of *Kentucky Is My Land*, Stuart illustrates the importance of dreaming, as a kind of future action, or action in rehearsal. The poem tells the story of Ben Tuttle who, as a child, dreams of being a great conquerer. But Ben Tuttle abandons his dream, for he does not want to be a destroyer of life. After witnessing the destruction of trees as the timber industry clears hills familiar to him, and seeing the subsequent erosion, Ben Tuttle begins to dream a different dream. He wants "To make earth better for his being here,/ To help his people always and never destroy./ Always to build, ever, ever, ever to build." So Ben Tuttle devotes his life to reclaiming the hurt land by planting trees. "He salted earth with sweat as years went by." He lives to see the fulfillment of his dream—in reforested land—and feels a sense of accomplishment knowing "He has given something to his people,/ To his country, his State and his Republic." Ben Tuttle believes his creation of a forest is as important as the work of a general, a writer, or a composer, for he has created beauty for people and made them "happier than/ They would have been had he not dreamed."

Stuart's "The Builder and the Dream" is an appropriate conclusion for *Kentucky Is My Land*. The poem is a fitting culmination of Stuart's preoccupation with the meaning of the country's pioneer and settlement phase, and with the themes of home, family, freedom, productive work, and growth. It illustrates his belief that one should make reality out of one's dreams. For like his fictional counterpart, Ben Tuttle, Jesse Stuart was both dreamer and doer; that is, he was typically American.

Without contradiction, Jesse Stuart is very much a Kentuckian and at the same time very American. Related philosophically to the New England Transcendentalists, of whom Ralph Waldo Emerson is perhaps the chief spokesman, Stuart shares Emerson's understanding of the relationship between word and thing. In his essay "Nature," Emerson says that words are "signs of natural facts" and that "particular natural facts are symbols of particular spiritual facts." The world that Jesse Stuart creates with words is a symbolic embodiment of a tradition, a symbol-at-large, which resonates with very American values and aspirations. Stuart blends his Kentucky background and experience with strains of American literary tradition and philosophical thought to produce poems that express American ideas, attitudes, values, and ideals.

Jesse Stuart is a poet in the truest sense. His mentor at Vanderbilt University, Donald Davidson, called him the first real poet, aside from the ballad-makers, to come out of the Appalachian mountain region, and in his person, life, and work Stuart reminds us of the true nature and function of the poet, and of the poet's relation to his place and people. The poet's works are not mere exercises in self-expression, as another of Stuart's teachers at Vanderbilt University, fellow Kentuckian Robert Penn Warren suggests. He says as much when he recalls Stuart as a young man in whom, it seemed, "all the life he had absorbed was struggling to find a way out, and perhaps to achieve its meaning." Stuart had absorbed the life of his people and place, his state and country, and as a consequence what he has to say is not merely his personal expression. The poet, as Emerson points out, is the "representative person," and in his role as "Sayer" gives expression not merely to his own thoughts and feelings and aspirations, but to those of others as well. The poet expresses the experience of a whole place and its people. This is certainly the case with Jesse Stuart, for he began to write when his part of the country was beginning to "say" itself, as Emerson would put it, and to express its meaning, its identity, its understanding of the past and present, and its hopes for the future, through its literature.

Instead of being mere personal expression, Stuart's poems are an expression of his land and people. In Stuart's created world of words we find not just his but our own thoughts, feelings, ideas, and aspirations. His language has the power to heighten our awareness of both the uniqueness and the universality of our exprience, to help us to appreciate not only who we are as Americans living in the Appalachian South, but to appreciate as well the universal element in our experience, the things we have in common with human beings of all times and places. Finally, Stuart reminds us that we are all children of the earth, that the earth is the very source of our lives.

This realization, this felt sense of being a child of the earth, is both a poetic insight and the most practical of considerations; and it accounts for both Stuart the poet, the "brother to trees," and for Stuart the conservationist. Here, too, Stuart stands in a very American tradition: His conservation ethic resembles that of Henry David Thoreau, also a poet who recognized the practical necessity of wilderness. And as a farmer and healer of hurt land, Stuart exemplifies the ideas of the Vanderbilt University Agrarians with whom he came in contact. Although Stuart was never a member of the Agrarian group, he has proved, as a student of his life and work, J. R. LeMaster, has said, "the most constant Agrarian of them all."

In his person, life, and work, Stuart is a representative man—a representative Kentuckian and a representative American. He was not the sort of trendy, fashionable writer who fancied himself too deep and sensitive to be understood. Stuart's work is accessible. He did not stand back from the common life; he plunged into it. During a long, productive life, he was a farmer, school teacher, high school principal, county superintendent, and, for a time, a newspaper editor. He was active in local civic affairs. Like Ben Tuttle in "The Builder and the Dream," he was also a far-sighted conservationist who planted over 20,000 trees on his land.

An outgoing, energetic man interested in everything and everybody, Stuart was as much at home in a cattle barn or at a tobacco sale as he was in the classroom, lecture hall, or at his desk. He was instinctively positive, an affirmer, as *Kentucky Is My Land,* on any page, bears out. Because he was both dreamer and doer, he turned his dreams into deeds and words. But he did not tear down. He was a builder—of barns, fences, land. And he was a builder with words.

Stuart understood that dreaming and doing, dreaming and building, are inseparable. There is a saying that goes: Back of the deed was the doer, back of the doer the dream. Jesse Stuart understood this progression, and this connection between dream and deed, ideal and reality. When he was presented with the award of the Academy of American Poets, in 1961, for "distinguished poetic achievement," he chose to read "Hold to a Living Dream," from *Kentucky Is My Land.*

Stuart's dreams did not turn him away from reality, or cause him to long for a golden past. As he says in "The Undefeated," one of the "Songs of a Mountain Plowman" in this volume, "Only defeated and those needing rest/ Recount the splendor of the sundown past/ In idle dreams, thinking it was the best." Stuart was an active, not an idle dreamer. For him "The future is a germinating seed" and "Time the Present is here now,/ The realistic dream we can't escape./ We hold it in our hand and when and how/ Will you and I forge it into a shape?"

Stuart knew whereof he spoke. He valued the past, and the example of our pioneer forebears. But he lived in the present, and worked for the future, forging his realistic dream into a desired shape. Just as Ben Tuttle's neighbors, observing how he reclaimed eroded land and created a forest on it, began to imitate him and to "model their future on Ben Tuttle's dream," Kentuckians—indeed, all Americans—can model for the future on the example of Jesse Stuart's life and work. *Kentucky Is My Land,* a work of the mature Jesse Stuart, is a good book through which to become acquainted with Stuart's life, work, and values, or with which to renew and deepen one's appreciation for the life of an outstanding Kentuckian and American who made "earth better for his being here."

Kentucky Is My Land is very much a book of its time. Most of these poems were written during World War II and immediately afterward, and published in magazines during the mid- and-late Forties and early Fifties. They first appeared as *Kentucky Is My Land* in September, 1952. The book was well received. A *Saturday Review* critic had special praise for "Elegy for Mitch Stuart" and for "The Ballad of Lonesome Waters." The reviewer for the *Chicago Sunday Tribune* called "The Builder and the Dream" "one of the few poems in praise of forest conservation that is really readable."

Stuart's expressions of patriotism, his example of willingness to sacrifice himself in the defense of freedom, his celebration of productive work, may be the themes that made the book seem timely over thirty years ago. Today, the other themes, his celebration of the land and the seasons, of home and family, show the book to possess an appeal that transcends any particular time or place. Like all good literature, *Kentucky Is My Land* is full of "news that stays news." It presents us with particular people, places, and circumstances in such a way that the new is seen under the aspect of the unchanging, while the unchanging is forever renewed. Reading it, we discover that *Kentucky Is My Land* is a book for our time, too, a book with a peculiar power to inspire us as we forge our dreams for our families, for our fellow Kentuckians and Americans, into desired shapes. For anyone able to say, along with Jesse Stuart, "Kentucky Is My Land," this is a book to take along into the future.

—Jim Wayne Miller

The Jesse Stuart Foundation

The Jesse Stuart Foundation was founded in 1979 as a public, non profit entity devoted to preserving both Jesse Stuart's literacy legacy and W-Hollow, the little valley made famous in his works. The Foundation, a regional press and bookseller, controls the rights to Stuart's works, and it is reprinting Stuart's out-of-print books along with other books that focus on Kentucky and Appalachia.

The 730-acre Stuart farm in W-Hollow, exclusive of the home place, was turned over to the Commonwealth of Kentucky by the Stuarts in 1980. It is now designated the "Jesse Stuart Nature Preserve" and is part of the Kentucky Nature Preserves System, with ownership vested in the Kentucky Nature Preserves Commission.

The Jesse Stuart Foundation is governed by a Board of Directors consisting of University presidents, members of the Stuart family, and leaders in business, industry, and government. The Foundation also has an Executive Director, who manages its day-to-day business, plans and schedules events and meetings, and coordinates publication projects.

Associate Memberships in the Foundation are available to the general public. Associate Members will receive a quarterly Newsletter, and a Stuart book or print as a membership gift.

For more information, contact:

The Jesse Stuart Foundation
P.O. Box 391
Ashland, KY 41114
(606) 329-5232